Hammock Camping

The Complete Guide to Greater Comfort, Convenience and Freedom

How to
Use, Make or Buy
A Camping Hammock

Ed Speer

Speer Hammocks, Inc.
Marion, North Carolina

All rights reserved. No part of this book may be reproduced or transmitted in any form or by any means, electronic or mechanical, including photocopying, recording or by any information storage and retrieval system, without written permission from the author, except for the inclusion of brief quotations in a review, which may be used with proper citation.

First Printing 2003
Second Printing 2003
Third Printing 2005
Copyright© 2003 Wade Edward Speer

Printed on acid-free recycled paper in the United States of America

Recycled Paper

Speer Hammocks, Inc.
34 Clear Creek Road
Marion, NC 28752-6407
828-724-4444
Email: info@speerhammocks.com
www.speerhammocks.com

Poems and quotations from Ditties, Copyright 2001 by N. Nomad used by permission of Eb Eberhart

Wilderness journal entries by Wade Edward Speer used by permission of Wade Edward Speer

Trademarks used in this book
Artiach® Casa Artiach, S.A.
Clear Seal™, Liquid Nails® Glidden Company
Coleman® The Coleman Co., Inc.
Crazy Crib™, Crazy Crib™ LE, Crazy Tarp™ Crazy Creek Products
Four Season Hammocks® Four Season Hammocks
Ozark Trail™ Stanlar Industries
Reflectix® Reflectix, Inc.
Ridge Rest®, Z-Rest™, Therm-A-Rest® Cascades Designs, Inc.
Thinsulate™, LiteLoft™ 3M Company
Silicone Water-Guard® Atsko, Inc.
Singer® The Singer Company Limited
Slumberjack® Slumberjack Products
Spectra® Honeywell Performance Fibers
Supplex®, Cordura® DuPont
The Clark Jungle Hammock® Clark Outdoor Products
Velcro® Velcro Industries B.V.

ISBN 0-9718594-4-2
LCCN 2002090866

Dedication

This book is dedicated to the memory of my dad, Clarence Gordon Speer, who not only taught me to love the outdoors, but who also designed and used his own innovative camping equipment.

The book is also dedicated to all outdoor travelers who seek to enhance their connection with nature....

Here's to all hearts of that cold, lonesome track,
*   To the life of the wanderlust...free.*
To all who have gone and have never come back,
*   Here's a tribute to you and to me.*

With our feet in the dirt we're the grit of the earth,
*   Heads aridin' the heavens o'erhead.*
And they won't find a nickel of value or worth,
*   When our fortunes are tallied and read.*

But no richer clan has there ever been known,
*   Since the times of all ruin and wrack;*
Than those of us lost to the dust outward blown,
*   Who have gone and have never come back.*

Nimblewill Nomad "LAND OF THE FREE"

Foreword

Over the past several decades, backpackers and campers alike have learned more than ever about comfort, technique and enjoyment in the outdoors.

In the mid and late-1990's, a number of newer backpacking techniques became publicized, emphasizing lighter gear and ways to travel in the wilderness that resulted in more freedom. Although there were many skeptics, these newer skills and techniques created a new breed of hiking enthusiasts.

These enthusiasts were hikers that began to create their own gear and experiment with radically different designs for lighter tents, stoves, backpacks, clothing, and other gear. Sometimes called "ultralite backpackers" or "gear heads", these hikers cut off the handles of their toothbrushes and the extra straps from their backpacks. They got rid of their 5-pound tents, their 4-pound sleeping bags, their 7-pound backpacks, and their heavy boots. Instead, they carried a tarp, an appropriate sleeping bag for the season, a pack that didn't weigh much more than a pound, and lightweight hiking shoes.

These "free-thinking" outdoor adventurers learned that they could hike comfortably with a lot less clothing and food than they first thought they needed. They'd rather be hiking up and down mountains with ease than becoming beasts of burden with a heavy pack. They felt that by carrying less weight they could reduce potential injuries. They could also cover more trail miles in a day and enjoy their trips more than ever. The benefits were endless! Comfort, health, ease of hiking, and enjoyment of the trip were far more important to them than the challenge of a heavy pack or being ready for the next blizzard of the century. They were able to eliminate their fears and macho attitudes and hike more enjoyably and realistically.

In the past several years, with the help of the Internet and word-of-mouth along the trails, this knowledge is being communicated more than ever. Those hikers that have barely ever set foot on a trail, those dreaming of a better experience in the outdoors, and those novice long-distance-hikers are now being provided years of trail-tested experience unlike ever before. They are getting their knowledge and increasing their enthusiasm for the outdoors from people like Ed Speer.

When I met Ed "Not-to-Worry" Speer for the first time, we were both in pursuit of hiking the entire length of the Appalachian Trail. He was carrying a 3/4-pound commercial "backpack", a stove of his own creation, and a hammock that he designed himself. His base pack weight (including all gear without food and water) was about 9 pounds, and when it was loaded with food and water it was rarely above 20 pounds. His pack was so small everyone thought he was a day-hiker, and you couldn't even see his pack when he was hiking toward you. At that time, few hikers on the trail were aware of the advantages of ultralight gear. Ed was an ultralight enthusiast if I'd ever seen one.

At the time I'd also been carrying similar gear, minus the hammock. Although I had been backpacking for over 20 years, I was able to learn lightweight techniques with the help of people sharing information on the Internet, and from encounters with rare outdoor adventurers like Ed. I fully believed that lighter was better, but I just didn't have enough miles of trail experience. I was carrying a stove of my own creation, a custom-made 2-pound tent, and the same 3/4-pound pack that Ed used. However, I wasn't able to squeeze my pack and gear down like Ed's to the same miniscule proportions. I didn't have quite the same flexibility, comfort, or multiple uses with my gear. Although I was

Foreword

happy with my gear, I wanted to do better. So I hiked with Ed on and off for several weeks, and our friendship grew out of common interests in backpacking and a similar analytical approach to gear.

I was amazed whenever we got to camp for the evening that Ed was always able to consistently set up in just a few minutes by strapping his hammock between a couple of trees. There were usually hundreds of trees to choose from and whenever a trail shelter or campsite was crowded or loud, he could easily set up just a little further away or hike a little more. He never had to worry about where to set up, since he had so many options!

I have hiked with Ed on several occasions since, and have learned plenty from his hammock camping techniques. Whenever we camped together, I was always the limiting factor, since I needed a clear and level area for my tent. It sometimes took me 15 to 20 minutes or longer to set up my tent because I needed to find or create an appropriate spot. I recall a camping spot near Pearisburg, VA that was particularly rocky, and I had great difficulty setting up my small tent. It was nearly dark and we had spent quite a bit of time hiking just to find a level spot. Ed set up his hammock in minutes while I took considerably longer to set up my tent. I ended up tossing and turning all night because of the rocks, sticks, roots, and uneven ground that I didn't even notice while setting up. I was too tired to notice or care. Needless to say, Ed slept a lot better in his hammock than I did that night in my tent.

After just a few experiences like this one, I realized that I needed to give hammock camping a try. That summer, I purchased and used a popular lightweight camping hammock for over 500 miles of the Appalachian Trail. Although I did enjoy it on several occasions, I was not as comfortable with it as I would have liked, and often got cold, especially in the alpine areas of the White Mountains in New Hampshire. After talking with Ed

Foreword

about the shortcomings of my poor hammock choice (specifically my 6' 4" height and how I was using the hammock), I've now learned what it takes to be comfortable sleeping in a properly fitted hammock, night after night.

The consistency of being able to find a camping location, regardless of terrain, brush, or wet ground is invaluable to the wilderness traveler or even the weekend camper. The environmental benefits are spectacular. Just knowing that I may have saved a salamander or not disturbed the home of an endangered plant or other critter makes me feel like I'm doing my part to help preserve our environment. Knowing that I didn't pitch my tent over a heavily used tent site (or possibly over someone's improperly disposed excrement!) makes me feel better. Knowing that I won't have to deal with unwanted critters throughout the night, and that I will have a consistently comfortable bed to sleep in gives me confidence. I have a newfound flexibility and freedom that I've never experienced before while backpacking.

There are many trends that are happening in our world today. Hammock camping is one that is picking up steam and is most certainly here to stay for the long term. Outdoor adventurers everywhere have a lot to learn from people like Ed. If you enjoy wilderness activities like camping, hiking, backpacking, canoeing, etc., take a serious look at hammock camping. I agree with Ed that once you try and learn the trail-tested techniques in this book, your outdoor adventures will take a major turn for the better.

Greg "G-Force" Scholz
AT 2000

Table of Contents

Good News! • Get off the Ground! • Freedom • No Trace Camping • Hammocks vs. Camping Hammocks • Comfort • Safety • Bugs • Storm Protection • Cold Weather Use • Multiple Uses • Lightweight • Make Your Own! • Buying a Hammock • Web Site • This Book is for You

Many People Doubt Comfort • Waterbed Cocoon in the Air • What About Tipping Over? • Toss and Turn? • Proper Size • How to Hang Hammock • Not too Tight • Adjusting Comfort • What About Wind? • Don't They Sag too Much? • Back-Sleeper Comfort • Fetal Position Sleepers • Nylon Fabrics • Lounge Chairs! • Hammock Tree Knots • Sound Sleep

Mountains • Hammocks on the Coast • Bears • Snakes • Other Animals • Rain • Use on the Ground • Rain Canopy • Rain Canopy Guidelines • New Freedom

Table of Contents

Table of Contents

Table of Contents

List of Illustrations

List of Illustrations

About the Author

Ed Speer has a long association with the outdoors. Growing up in the mountains of western North Carolina only wetted his appetite for outdoor adventure. His parents were avid campers who took him on many outdoor trips. Before long, he was leading his own trips into the wilderness and  spending more and more time in the outdoors. By his college years, he was an accomplished backcountry traveler who was comfortably hiking, camping, canoeing, rock climbing, fishing and caving throughout the US.

Ed turned his love of the outdoors into a career as an exploration geologist, which greatly expanded his time outside. Earning Geology degrees from the Universities of Missouri and Arizona led to work assignments throughout the western and southern United States, as well as parts of Canada, South America, and Africa. Ed's successful career focused on gold and diamond exploration.

After years of acquiring the necessary skills, Ed turned to epic outdoor adventures, including a 1,600-mile solo kayak trip along the west coast of Canada and Alaska. In the past three years, he has hiked over 5,000 miles on the Appalachian Trail, including two complete hikes from end to end. Ed's trail name, "Not To Worry," aptly reflects his philosophy of nature.

Ed has retired in order to spend more time in his beloved outdoors and to pursue his writing interests.

Preface

The idea and encouragement for this book comes from my outdoor friends who, over many years, have expressed a strong interest in my unique camping system. During a wide variety of outdoor adventures, they have immediately recognized the convenience and freedom of my hammock system, and were surprised but delighted to learn how extremely comfortable it is. Often they envied the ease and comfort I enjoyed with my "waterbed in the air," while all too often their tent or tarp use became an unpleasant ordeal. In all types of weather and terrain I enjoyed dry, warm and comfortable nights while they struggled less successfully.

While others tented in crowded or abused campsites, I pitched my hammock in never-used stealth sites deep in the forest or on mountain highs, often with exceptional views. While others frequently settled for uneven or rocky beds, I slept comfortably above those obstacles. While others were restricted to the few established backcountry campsites, I had millions of suitable sites from which to choose. While others struggled in cold exposed tent sites, I pitched my hammock out of the wind below a ridgeline or behind a rock cliff. While others had no option but to contribute to the overuse of backcountry campsites by their presence, I pitched my hammock away from the traveled path and in greater harmony with nature. While others often encountered camp-robbing critters, accustomed to easy food at established campsites, I unobtrusively shared the forest with all animals and never had to worry about unpleasant animal encounters.

This book is for all those who dream of a better way to do what they already love--outdoor adventure.

Preface

I bring a lifetime of outdoor experience to the task, including over 10,000 miles of solo wilderness travel by foot and paddle. My career as a geologist has also added greatly to my outdoor expertise. I've tested and refined my hammock camping in such diverse places as the jungles of South America, the Everglades of Florida, the Okefenokee Swamp of Georgia, the 2,000-mile Appalachian Trail from Georgia to Maine, the rugged Southern Appalachian Mountains including Mt. Mitchell in North Carolina, the rocky coasts of British Columbia and Alaska, as well as dozens of similar places.

My interest in hammock camping began 14 years ago on a six-month trip in unfamiliar bear country. This was a 1,600-mile solo kayak trip along the west coast of British Columbia and Alaska. I was going to be in the habitat of the aggressive Brown Bear, especially their coastal feeding grounds. While heeding the standard warnings to "Hang your food," I decided to hang myself out of the reach of the bears as well! Thus was born my interest in camping hammocks.

I succeeded that summer and avoided the many coastal bears! But I often hung my hammock high in the trees or from rock ledges using climbing equipment. Although my system was heavy, bulky and far from comfortable, the idea was born--hammocks can be incredibly convenient in the wilderness. Over the ensuing years, I've bought, tested, made and developed numerous hammocks seeking lighter weight and greater sleep comfort. Although slow in coming, the answers were incredibly simple--that's what this book is all about.

A properly made one-person camping hammock can be lightweight, strong and comfortable while still providing a complete camping shelter with a bug net and rain canopy. Weighing only two or three pounds, the hammock makes an ideal outdoor shelter for the adventure traveler camping in forested terrain. Whether you are car camping, family camping, or roaming the backcountry, hammocks can enrich your adventure.

The really good news is that you can make your own! With only a sewing machine and about $100 in mail-order materials, even the novice can make his/her own camping hammock superior to many commercial models. This book tells you how.

For those not inclined to tackle a make-your-own project, I also review the suitable camping hammocks currently available for purchase; there are only a few, including my custom-made hammocks.

Hammock camping developments are happening rapidly as more and more people are taking hammocks to the backcountry. Everyone can keep up on the latest by visiting the Hammock Camping Web Site: **www.HammockCamping.com**.

It is my hope and vision that this book introduces people to the freedom and joy of hammock camping. It gives me great satisfaction to share my ideas and bring more outdoor enjoyment to my fellow travelers while at the same time reducing our collective adverse impact on the wilderness.

Not To Worry

Ed Speer

Acknowledgments

Many people have contributed significantly to this book. Field discussions and reviews of early drafts have been invaluable and I owe many thanks to the people who gave freely of their time and opinions.

The numerous discussions I've had with others while on wilderness trips have been particularly enlightening and encouraging. After hearing about or actually seeing me use my unique camping system, many people asked questions or suggested alternatives. From these comments, I've not only improved my hammock camping system but I've learned that it is also suitable for many of my fellow travelers. In addition, I've found encouragement to share my ideas with others. Over the years, everyone who has shown an interest in my hammock has helped contribute to this book. Thanks to all of my fellow travelers who have shared their ideas.

Editorial reviews by fellow long-distance hikers were particularly helpful. These include those by: Greg "G-Force" Scholz of Farmington, CT; Stacy "Mother Hen" Hielinger of Baltimore, MD; Tim "Sherpa" Johnson of New York, and Matthew "DS" Carter of Louisville, KY. Additional helpful reviews include those by: Dr. Cato and Susan Holler and their son Chris, all of Marion, NC; Shanon and Sarah Wood of Lenoir, NC; Scott Speer of Paulies Island, SC; and Andrea Robinson of Louisville, KY.

Grammar editing by Mary "Tish" Ebling of Spruce Pine, NC enhanced the readability of the book and saved me innumerable embarrassments. Any remaining problems are mine alone. Thanks Tish for a difficult job well done.

Acknowledgments

My sister Clarissa "Kessa" Speer of Spruce Pine, NC is an accomplished self-taught seamstress and her skill with a sewing machine is evident in all my hammocks. Thanks Kessa for all your hard work, suggestions and improvements; none of this would be possible without you.

Shanon Wood of Lenoir, NC graciously drew many of the diagrams throughout the book.

Eb "Nimblewill Nomad" Eberhart of Dahlonega, GA, who is an accomplished adventure traveler, gave permission to use his "trail" poetry throughout the book.

Warning-Disclaimer

The information in this book is provided in the spirit of sharing experiences with the hope that doing so will educate and entertain readers, as well as enhance their enjoyment of the outdoors. It is the purpose of this book to complement, amplify and supplement information available from other sources.

Every effort has been made to make this book as complete and accurate as possible. There may however, be typographical or content mistakes. The information in this book should therefore be used only as a general guide.

While great effort has been taken to provide sound advice, neither the author nor the publisher can be held responsible for any person or entity with respect to any loss or damage caused, or alleged to have been caused, directly or indirectly, by the information contained in this book.

If you do not wish to be bound by the above, you may return this book to the publisher for a refund.

Introduction
Who Is This Book For?

There's a journ' that leads to happiness,
Past the beaten path we know.
It's on our list called "one of these days,"
But we never stop...to go.

Nimblewill Nomad "ONE OF THESE DAYS"

Welcome to the exciting new world of hammock camping! Obviously you are reading this book because of your curiosity; maybe you've already considered hammocks, but didn't know where to go for more information. Whether you want to make your own hammock, buy an existing one, or just want to know how to use the new camping hammocks, this book is for you.

Everyone who loves and travels in the backcountry will find this book useful.

Good News!

A properly made camping hammock is like a "waterbed cocoon in the air." It's as comfortable as a waterbed; and, like a cozy cocoon, it is a complete secure shelter. Of course you are skeptical, but keep reading!

24 - Hammock Camping

One of my biggest reasons for going to the wilderness, and probably one of yours too, is to "smooth it." It's certainly not to "rough it". Camping hammocks are a major step in that direction. Sleeping in a hammock has a soothing and royal quality that is lacking in the more conventional outdoor habit of sleeping on the ground. Chapter 1, "The Joy and Comfort of Hammock Camping," is for everyone who seeks greater comfort in the backcountry.

Get off the Ground!

So, get off the ground for a truly comfortable night sleeping in the outdoors! Forget about crawling around on your hands and knees and coping with rocks, roots, brush, and wet or uneven ground beneath your bed. Forget snakes, slugs, spiders, bees, ticks, logs, mud, briers, cacti, poisonous plants, rats, mice, chipmunks, dogs, cats, foxes, rabbits, squirrels, raccoons, and even porcupines!

Sleeping in the air puts you above these problems. Anyone who has ever had to deal with free-roaming dogs, or even other campers' pets, will also appreciate the security of a hammock. This book is for everyone who wants to say goodbye to unwanted camp critters.

Freedom

Hammock camping is fun, comfortable, and extremely convenient. Chapter 2, "The Convenience of Hammock Camping," should convince you. Imagine the freedom of making camp where you want, rather than the typical crowded and/or overused tent campsites. The possibilities are unlimited in forested terrain where literally millions of suitable sites beckon the hammock camper. In fact, the vast majority of our wilderness destinations are forested and thus suitable for hammock camping. For hammock use in treeless areas, see the alternate ideas presented elsewhere in this book.

No Trace Camping

Hammocks reduce, and can even eliminate, the overuse and abuse so typical of many of our backcountry tent campsites. A properly used hammock leaves no adverse impact on the environment and is the ultimate Leave No Trace camping shelter. I've devoted an entire chapter to this issue: Chapter 4, "Hammock Camping is Environmentally Friendly," explains hammocks as a better way to travel in the backcountry. If you are interested in reducing your wilderness impact, this book can help.

Not all hammocks however, are suitable for our use. While many comfortable hammocks are available on the market today, only a few qualify as suitable camping hammocks. This book will help you find the right one.

The overnight or extended backcountry traveler demands more from a hammock than the backyard user. He/She must have a dependable shelter, one that provides adequate protection from the various conditions encountered or expected during the outing. Only a very small number of hammocks available for purchase today meet the wilderness travelers' needs. In this book, you will find reviews of these hammocks (Chapter 7) plus make-your-own instructions for a highly successful, field-tested hammock (Chapter 6).

Hammocks vs. Camping Hammocks

Many hammocks can be adapted for wilderness use by adding a rain tarp and a bug net. Ordinary hammocks and suitable camping hammocks however, can be distinguished on the basis of:

26 - Hammock Camping

1) Comfort
2) Safety
3) Bugs
4) Storm Protection
5) Multiple uses
6) Lightweight

Some explanation is necessary.

Comfort

While there are many advantages to hammock camping, comfort is at the top of my list. The hammock designs in this book are extremely comfortable. This comfort is a feature of the hammocks' design, i.e., their shape, size and fabric. Proper hanging, which is easily mastered, is also critical to user comfort.

The extended outdoor traveler never knows when he/she might be delayed in camp and confined to the hammock for periods of time longer than overnight. I once spent 36 hours in my hammock while storm bound on a lake in Boundary Waters in northern Minnesota. On another occasion, high winds prevented me from leaving a small sea island in the Florida Everglades for two days. In both cases, the camp time was spent comfortably lounging in the hammock and reading a good book. Similar camp time in a tent or under a tarp on the ground quickly becomes an unpleasant ordeal.

Safety

Safety in a hammock is obviously critical. No one can rest, much less sleep, in a hammock while worried about being dumped on the ground. When occupied, my hammock is designed to hang below its center of gravity; therefore it is not prone to tip over. In fact, it takes extra effort to get out of it! In addition, the hammock materials, while being lightweight, are selected and tested to be strong enough to carry the occupant's weight without instilling fear of failure. Chapter 5, "Hammock Camping Safety," explains some safety concerns of interest to all hammock users.

Bugs

The adequate camping hammock should have suitable bug protection. My hammock has a bug proof solid fabric bottom and no-see-um bug netting on top. More than once I've been driven into my hammock by hoards of mosquitoes, no-see-ums, or biting black flies. It's nice to know my hammock offers protection while still being comfortable. The net can be easily detached on either side for getting in or out, or for using the hammock as a handy lounge chair!

The bug net is certainly nice to have during bug season; however, it's not always necessary. For those times when bugs are not a problem, the net can be removed and left at home. On a recent seven-month hike, I slept without the bug net more than 70% of the time. The bug net weighs about six ounces, which is significant to backpackers concerned with reducing pack weight.

Storm Protection

Adequate rain protection is also important to the comfort of a camping hammock. My hammock has a wide rain canopy that extends well beyond the hammock itself. This makes a surprisingly practical stand-up shelter! The eight-by-ten foot canopy provides ample rain and wind protection while allowing the camper to be outside the hammock itself. This is convenient for sitting in the hammock, getting in or out of the hammock, changing clothes while standing, loading or unloading the pack, and even cooking a meal! If really foul weather is expected, the canopy can be lowered for even more protection.

28 - Hammock Camping

Cold Weather Use

Hammocks become less comfortable as the temperature drops, eventually reaching a point at which it is warmer to sleep on the ground. The adequate camping hammock system therefore, like mine, must provide for sleeping on the ground. It's probably best to avoid hammocks in sub-zero temperatures unless you are willing to carry considerable additional weight in insulating gear.

Multiple Uses

My hammock system is multi-use and designed for ground use should adequate supports not be available or the temperatures unexpectedly drop below my comfort level. At such times, the hammock becomes a bivy sack and the canopy is pitched just as a normal tarp would be.

Some of my trail-tested gear and techniques however, can safely extend the cold weather use of the hammock. Insulating sleep pads and sleeping bags rigged around the hammock can be used to keep warm as the seasonal, storm or alpine temperatures unexpectedly drop. This is such an important innovation that an entire chapter is devoted to staying warm; everything you need to know can be found in Chapter 3, "How To Stay Warm."

Lightweight

Weighting only two to three pounds, camping hammocks offer an obvious advantage over heavier tents. There simply is no better way to lighten one's pack weight without compromising camp comfort, security or convenience.

The features mentioned above are covered in more detail elsewhere in this book. It is these features, born of actual backcountry experience, that make my hammock camping system uniquely suited for the adventure traveler.

Make Your Own!

You too can make your own highly practical camping hammock following the directions given in this book. Chapter 6, "How To Make Your Own Hammock" gives you everything you need to know. Make your own complete hammock camping system and start enjoying the backcountry all over again.

Buying a Hammock

Not interested in making your own hammock? You can still participate in the new camping system by purchasing a camping hammock. Chapter 7, "How To Buy a Hammock," has everything you need to know to make a wise decision.

Web Site

For more information on hammock camping, check out the following web site: **www.hammockcamping.com**.

Additional Information

Appendix 1 lists the unique features of the Speer complete wilderness hammock camping solution. Appendix 2 summarizes information given elsewhere in this book. Appendix 3 lists some of the numerous Internet sources for hammock information, manufactures, sellers and users. Appendix 4 explains some of the Leave No Trace principles for wise outdoor use.

30 - Hammock Camping

This Book is for You

Whether you are looking for a general use camping hammock with secure comfort in mind or an extremely lightweight one for marathon hiking, this book will help. Whether you decide to purchase a hammock or make your own, all the information can be found here. Whether you are looking for tips on how or where to use a hammock, how to stay warm in a hammock, or how to camp more in harmony with nature, this book is your ultimate guide to happily hoisting yourself off the ground.

Never sleep on the ground again and you can forget about snakes and spiders

Chapter 1
The Joy and Comfort of Hammock Camping

Are hammocks really comfortable? As hard as it may be to believe, comfort is my number one reason for carrying a hammock. Most people agree that my hammock is far more comfortable than any bed they've ever had on the ground!

Of course, the correct answer to the above question is: "Some are, some aren't." I've found that a hammock's comfort is dependent on: 1) the design, meaning its shape, size and fabric; and 2) how it is pitched. This chapter examines the importance of each of these features in providing comfort suitable for the adventure traveler. The good news is you can easily buy or make your own extremely comfortable hammock that is ideal for extended wilderness use!

Many People Doubt Comfort

Most people are rightly doubtful of hammock comfort given their experience; the problem lies in the hammocks they have tried. At least in the US, we have been overly exposed to poorly designed commercial hammocks, such as some of the universal string net hammocks with or without spreader bars. Almost everyone has tried and rejected them. Certainly many excellent net hammocks are available. However, most adventure travelers have limited their trials to poorly made ones, with the expected poor results.

Lightweight string net hammocks intrigue me too. Their great strength and low weight suggest they might be suitable for serious wilderness use. However, they miserably fail my comfort test. Their excessive stretch and sag results in cramping shoulder squeeze and back bend that make them uncomfortable for sleeping. No wonder people's experience makes them suspicious of my claims of superior comfort in my hammock.

I, too, was a victim of poorly designed hammocks until the promise of a really comfortable camping hammock and my curiosity led me to making my own. I now realize that properly made hammocks are extremely comfortable. My hammock has evolved from years of trying different fabrics, shapes and sizes in actual wilderness conditions. The result is a remarkably practical and comfortable camping hammock system.

Waterbed Cocoon in the Air

In fact, I call my camping hammock a "waterbed cocoon in the air." It's as comfortable as a waterbed and, like a cocoon, it is a complete secure shelter!

What About Tipping Over?

Many hammocks are unsuitable for the wilderness traveler, not because they are uncomfortable, but because they are too heavy to carry easily or they lack the required bug and rain protection. Others are actually dangerous and can easily tip over; this is less of a problem in the back yard than it is in the wilderness. In fact, spreader bars, which are often used in an attempt to correct an otherwise poor hammock design, can make a hammock unstable by raising the user's center of gravity, which can lead to tipping over. Note that after some recent accidents involving young children, most string net hammocks sold in the US now employ spreader bars; but this can make them even more unsuitable for wilderness use.

Considering some of the rugged places where I now camp, such as atop rock cliffs or on steep mountainsides, tipping over must certainly be avoided! Therefore, most string net hammocks with spreader bars are best left at home.

However, properly designed solid fabric hammocks without spreader bars, like mine, can evenly support the user's weight safely below the center of gravity, and provide remarkable comfort--like an aerial waterbed! The best designs originated hundreds, if not thousands, of years ago! All I've done is mate modern materials with these ancient designs. The modern materials, such as solid nylon fabrics, no-see-um bug netting, hook and loop attachment strips, low-tangle lines, and low-memory-stretch polypropylene straps, are lightweight while giving superior performance.

Toss and Turn?

Many people express their concern about hammock sleeping this way: "But I toss and turn all night long," insinuating they would not be able to sleep well in a hammock. However, the exact opposite actually happens in a properly made hammock! The hammock sleeper does not toss and turn excessively because there is no need to do so; my hammock supports the body much better than the unyielding ground or even a bed with a mattress. As remarkable as this sounds, it is true. The hammock sleeper remains comfortable all night long without suffering from the usual hip and/or shoulder pressure points common to beds, mattresses and sleep pads on the ground. In addition, the hammock responds to the sleeper's every move, continually readjusting and eliminating any pressure points before they cause discomfort.

The first-time user often finds that the continually readjusting hammock is limiting his/her ability to turn over or even move inside the hammock. However, the proper technique of gripping the hammock edges to provide leverage is quickly learned and soon becomes second nature.

Proper Size

Hammocks must also be sized properly for real sleeping comfort. This means sufficient length and width, which are often lacking in many commercially available hammocks that are mass-produced with cost-saving shortcuts. These too-short and too-narrow hammocks can be quite unsuitable for the average sleeper, and especially unsuitable for extended trips. They are also unsuitable for the big or tall user. Buying or making your own customized hammock guarantees compatibility for you and the wilderness.

While all hammock design features are interrelated and it's generally inaccurate to single out only one feature, I will do so here in order to make a point. Generally, a long hammock is more comfortable than a short one. I've found that the minimum length for sleep comfort is at least two feet longer than the user's height. Thus a six-foot tall camper should have an eight-foot long hammock.

I've also settled on a width of five feet to efficiently hold an adult and his/her sleeping bag and sleep pad. This allows for deep sides in the occupied hammock and eliminates the fear of falling out.

Joy and Comfort

McKenzie Lake, Quetico Provincial Park, Ontario, Canada
Jun 13, 2000

What a gorgeous wilderness lake! Numerous islands dot this large lake, while rocky shores lend a glacial beauty. Hoards of mosquitoes infest the trees and brush along the shore, so I've set up on an island. My first choice island has an occupied eagle's nest, so I've taken an adjacent island. My hammock is pitched in trees on a rocky outcrop where winds can keep mosquitoes away. No one has ever camped here before. Fly-fishing with surface poppers was deadly on the small mouth bass today; fishing doesn't get much better than this. From my hammock I watch eagles, loons, ducks, and gulls. Two deer swim across the lake at dusk. Earlier today I watched a moose maneuvering through thick brush.

Graveyard Creek, Everglades National Park, FL
Dec 13, 1994

What a blessed relief to finally be in my hammock, gently swaying in the sea breezes! It was a long, hard paddle today against constant headwinds and waves; there were no places to get out of the canoe and stretch. I thought my back would surely break before we could get here. An hour in the hammock has me feeling much better. For the first time, I notice the very noisy Kingfisher who is repeatedly diving underwater for his dinner, the large flock of White Ibis feeding on the shallow mud bank, and the Great Blue Heron fishing along the nearby creek bank.

Mountain To Sea Trail, Linville Mountain, NC
Aug 17, 2000

The climb up from the North Fork River was long and difficult, but the views from Bald Knob and Mt. Dodson were worth it. With millions of trees to choose from, finding a campsite is easy and my hammock goes up quickly. Even though the trail is seldom used, I choose a site well away from the path. The hammock hangs above rocks on the rugged ridge top and I have an unparalleled view of the North Cove valley to the west. I fix my dinner on the rocks and retire to the hammock to watch the setting sun. The nearest tent campsite is miles away.

Although sizes smaller than these are common to many hammocks, they generally compromise comfort and safety.

The eight-by-five foot hammock design in this book is sized for my six-foot tall, 170-pound body. Undoubtedly, this is sufficient for many people; however, the design can easily be adjusted to accommodate shorter, taller, lighter, or heavier folks with little or no additional work or cost. Thus the hammock can be customized to users' specific requirements; everything you need is clearly explained in Chapter 6, "How To Make Your Own Hammock."

How to Hang Hammock

Comfort is also dependent on the proper hanging of the hammock, which can be quickly mastered. In the following discussion, a distinction is made between two types of "sag": 1) good sag, that which is sufficient to allow the user to hang well below the tip-over point; and 2) bad sag, that which is excessive between supports too close together and which prevents the user from lying horizontally.

Proper Hammock Setup

To properly pitch a hammock, select sturdy supports, generally trees, four to eight feet farther apart than the length of the hammock itself; then position the hammock evenly between the supports. Note that this means the average eight-foot hammock should be set up between supports that are 12 to 16 feet apart; that's a lot farther apart than most people would normally choose.

The object here is to have two-foot to four-foot long tie-outs on each end of the suspended hammock. In general, the farther apart the supports, the more level the hammock will be when occupied. Many purchased hammocks provide inappropriately short tie-out lines, which require supports too close together and result in excessive and uncomfortable sag when occupied; this is the best-avoided deep-V-shape common to many commercial hammocks. The twelve-foot long tie-outs designed for my hammock help ensure pitching with proper sag as long as the supports are four to eight feet farther apart than the length of the hammock itself, as called for above.

The tie-outs should also be attached to the supports at the same height above the ground; this is often an optical illusion problem on steeply sloping ground!

Not too Tight

On the other hand, the unoccupied hammock should not be set up pulled tightly between the supports, which will result in uncomfortable shoulder squeeze as well as an unnerving tipsy feeling. This tipsy feeling happens when the occupied hammock hangs too close to its center of gravity. It needs sufficient sag so your butt (your body's center of weight when lying in the hammock) is well below the tip-over level.

38 - Hammock Camping

Notice how the hammock ergonomically contours to the user's body. No more pressure points; this is comfort fit for a king!

Proper Hammock Support

The tip-over level of any hammock can be effectively visualized as the centerline between the ends of the occupied hammock. Therefore, the closer one's body is lying to the hammock's centerline, the more danger there is of tipping over and the more tipsy it feels, in much the same way as an unstable canoe feels tipsy. Being worried about getting dumped out is not conducive to a good night's sleep. Avoid pitching the hammock too tightly.

Pitching the hammock loosely and with the long tie-outs as described above helps ensure the proper degree of sag of the unoccupied hammock; this is safer and gives more interior space without compromising comfort. Too much sag here is better than too little. The amount of this sag is not critical as long as the tie-outs are sufficiently long and your butt doesn't hit the ground when you get in the hammock. You will soon learn to judge the proper amount of sag when pitching the hammock; just remember to use wide supports and don't pitch the hammock stretched so tightly that it is level with the tie-out attachment points.

Proper Hammock Height

With experience, you will soon take notice of slight differences in how the hammock is hanging. Once occupied, even a perfectly centered hammock as described above will hang lower at the head end than at the foot end since your head and upper torso are heavier than your feet (at least mine are). Generally this is not a problem and may not even be noticed by the user.

In addition, if the two tie-outs are not the same length, the end with the longer tie-out will hang lower than the shorter end; a similar pattern results if the two tie-outs are attached at different heights above the ground.

Adjusting Comfort

These features can actually be used to adjust the hammock for one's personal preferences. For instance, I prefer to have my foot end slightly higher than my head end since it helps the blood circulation in my poor feet after a long day of hiking. It also prevents my usual sliding toward the foot end of the hammock over the course of the night. Therefore I often raise my foot end tie-out a few inches and/or shorten it. Caution: While adding to my comfort, this has had disastrous effects when using my pee bottle during the night......!

What About Wind?

Contrary to popular belief, wind does not cause much swinging of the hammock, at least not nearly enough to suit me! This is unfortunate because gentle swaying in the air is especially soothing and conducive to relaxing! Rocking in my hammock is a much-anticipated joy at the end of a long day. What's good for the baby in the cradle is good for the tired camper in the hammock!

I'm not talking about using the hammock like a yard swing; it is not designed for such vigorous swinging and doing so is dangerous and could cause serious injury should something give way (and it probably will). However, gentle swaying should be safe. I generally position my hiking pole within easy reach so I can grab it and gently rock myself; nothing else solicits more attention, or more snickers, from my fellow campers! But what do I care-I'm soon sleeping like a baby!

Of course, hiding from cold wind is one of the greatest advantages of using a hammock in the first place. Generally I avoid as much wind as I can by setting up behind ridge crests or rock cliffs. See more about hiding from the wind in Chapter 3, "How To Stay Warm."

Don't They Sag too Much?

Still not convinced, many people also ask me, "Don't hammocks sag too much to be comfortable to sleep in?" Of course, we are now talking about the sag of the occupied hammock; the deep-V-shape all too common to many hammocks immediately comes to mind. The correct answer is, "No, a properly designed and pitched hammock will contour to the occupant's body and provide horizontal support!" It's really a matter of fabric, hammock size, and the length of the tie-outs. Yes, a horizontal position is possible!

Back-Sleeper Comfort

In my hammock, the back sleeper can fully stretch out in complete comfort! The extra length of my hammock allows one to stretch out along the centerline with only a minor bend in the middle. This is not the deep-V-shaped sag common to less well-designed hammocks. In fact this slight bend actually relieves pressure on the lower back and can add remarkable comfort compared to lying on the ground or in a bed. Yes, even more comfort! I've often suffered from lower back pain after several hours of sleeping on beds or in tents; my hammock is so effective at eliminating the cause of this pain, I now sleep in it all the time, even at home! The fully extended back-sleeper position is so comfortable that most people report that they must surely be lying perfectly horizontal; they don't even notice the slight bend!

Head and shoulders on the right
Feet on the left

Back Sleeper in Hammock

However, the back sleeper has another even more comfortable option. By positioning one's extended body slightly diagonal to the length of the hammock, one can be perfectly horizontal with no back bend! I told you it was possible! This diagonal position is only slightly off the centerline of the hammock. Moving one's feet and head only a few inches (8-12) in opposite directions is all that's required for this remarkably comfortable position. However, many hammocks, unlike mine, are too narrow to allow this diagonal position. I often sleep much of the night like this on my back.

Fetal Position Sleepers

There's also good news for fetal-position sleepers. Like most people, I, too, enjoy sleeping on my side with my knees pulled up. The hammock immediately adjusts to this new position and my body rests on a slight uniform incline from my butt to my head. The incline is comfortable and conducive to sleep; many doctors recommend just such a remedy for acid reflux sufferers (like I am). In this fetal sleeping position, my body is essentially occupying only half of the hammock length, from the low sag point to my head. Obviously, a hammock too short to allow this half-hammock position would be inappropriate for all night use.

Sleeping on my belly is the only position I've found that is not comfortable in my hammock; however, some people report no problem. A more suitable hammock for the belly sleeper can probably be made, although I've never tried. It would most likely need to be considerably longer (or wider?) than my design.

Note that the sleeper is occupying only half of the hammock's length
Head on the left, knees on the right

Fetal Position Sleeper in Hammock

Nylon Fabrics

The solid fabric of my hammock not only distributes weight evenly, but also adds to comfort by efficiently managing air and moisture. In the summer, the breathable fabric freely passes air in both directions and helps prevent the buildup of condensation in the sleeping bag, helping keep me cool and dry. Experience has taught me that heavily-coated fabrics, in combination with the bug net, cause unpleasant clamminess and even excessive condensation inside the hammock. Yes, the no-see-um bug net can block enough air to cause condensation inside the hammock, especially in combination with non-breathable bottom fabrics. Therefore, breathable hammock fabric is preferable, at least for summer use.

However, when storm, seasonal or alpine cold temperatures are expected, my first line of defense is to seal the fabric with silicone or durable water-resistant treatments to help retain warm air inside the hammock and prevent cold air from entering through the bottom. This is highly effective against cold wind without adding significant weight. See Chapter 3, "How To Stay Warm," for more on the use of fabric treatments.

Generally, these cooler temperatures, which are often drier and accompanied by more air movement, do not cause serious condensation or clamminess problems even though the fabric is now sealed against the passage of air. Note that the bug net is generally left at home in these colder, insect-free conditions; this provides greater airflow inside the hammock and helps solve the condensation problems of warm weather. Now that the bottom of the hammock is sealed against the passage of cold air, a sleeping bag is called on to block cold air on the top.

With the return of warm weather, the vapor-proof treatments are easily removed by washing the hammock using any detergent and fabric softener. It may take multiple washings to fully remove the treatments; wash your hammock only in front-loading tumbler-type machines to avoid tangling the straps and lines. In this way, the same hammock functions in both cold and hot weather. However, additional measures are often necessary to stay warm in cold weather-see Chapter 3, "How To Stay Warm."

For additional warmth, appropriate sleeping bags and/or sleep pads can be used in the hammock (again, see the "How To Stay Warm" chapter for specifics). A small pillow made from spare clothes in a carry sack completes the comfort of my airbed.

Lounge Chairs!

Hammocks can also double as the ultimate wilderness lounge chairs! Talk about royal camp luxury! Tents or tarps don't even come close. The bug net on my hammock easily detaches from either side to allow use as a lounge chair. Simply detach the bug net on one side, flip it over the hammock, and let it hang from the backside. The bug net support line also detaches and can be lowered over the backside out of the way.

Imagine sitting comfortably without getting on the ground. You can completely forget about creepy crawlers, rocks, logs, mud, wet ground, those pesky "stickers, " briers, cacti, and even poisonous plants! Everyone in the outdoors soon runs into these unpleasant characters and learns to avoid them with a passion. The hammock user also avoids rats, mice, chipmunks, dogs, cats, foxes, rabbits, squirrels, raccoons, and porcupines! With a hammock, your worries are over and you can relax in peace.

Hammock as Lounge Chair

Nothing else feels quite as good as relaxing in this remarkably comfortable chair at the end of a long day of hiking or canoeing. You can sit and remove your shoes, eat a snack, write in your journal, read a book, or just be quiet and listen to the sounds of the forest. Of course, such relaxation often turns into full-fledged power naps! With little effort, you can raise your feet, twist into the hammock and recline in divine comfort. With a few gentle swings of the hammock, it's sandman time. You'll never find this kind of relaxation on the ground!

Hammock Tree Knots

Knots should be easy to tie and untie. Above all, they should not damage the trees. This calls for a special multi-wrap, overlapping knot that tightens against the tree without locking tightly against itself. Low-memory-stretch polypropylene webbing straps are well suited for the task. Support trees at least four inches in diameter are ideal for the four-wrap knot described below. To tie the knot, follow the six steps below and refer to the picture sequence.

a) Grab a strap at the point you want it attached to the tree. The strap from your hand to the loose end of the strap is called the "bitter end." The strap from your hand back to the hammock is called the "standing line." Now hold your hand with the strap to the center of the tree.

b) First Wrap: While holding the standing line to the tree, make the first wrap around the tree with the bitter end, bringing it back to the front of the tree.

c) Second Wrap: Loop the bitter end over and around the standing line and make the second wrap around the tree going in the opposite direction of the first wrap, bringing the bitter end back to the front of the tree.

d) Third Wrap: Again, loop the bitter end over and around the standing line and make the third wrap around the tree going in the opposite direction of the second wrap; the standing line should now stay put without having to hold it.

e) Fourth Wrap: Now make the fourth wrap completely around the tree going in the same direction as the third wrap. Note: If sufficient strap is available, additional wraps can be beneficial, especially if the support is less than four inches in diameter.

f) To complete the knot, pass the bitter end between the last wrap and the tree in such a way that the last wrap tightens against the strap of the bitter end and holds it tightly to the tree. Keeping all of the wraps flat against the tree, without any twists in the strap, ensures better gripping power of the knot.

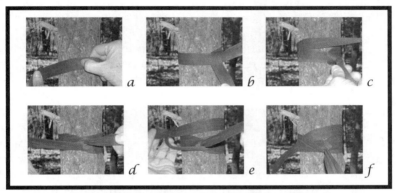

Four-Wrap Hammock Tree Knot

Notice that there is really nothing to untie since the straps press flat against the tree and each other. To undo, simply unwrap the straps. The idea is that the flat webbing wraps distribute the strain over a large area and tighten against the tree, with the last wrap securing the bitter end against the tree. When loaded, the flat webbing straps do not "roll" down the tree, thereby eliminating the bruises and scars to the bark of young trees commonly caused by the round ropes used on many hammocks.

Modifications of this multi-wrap knot can be used if there is insufficient strap length. Just remember, the more wraps the better the knot works. If you are forced to tie a tight knot in the strap itself, remember it will tighten greatly when loaded and may be impossible to untie. Prevent this by inserting a stick or a large fold of the loose end of the strap into the knot before adding your weight to the hammock.

48 - Hammock Camping

Sound Sleep

I sleep so soundly in my hammock that I'm often left out of the morning-after camp conversations. My fellow campers are amazed that I wake up only for the more severe or loudest rain shower, storm, or some other such nighttime disturbance. I sleep right through most of them!

Extended afternoon breaks also lend themselves well to setting up the hammock for some real rest. On one memorable hiking trip in Vermont, I was particularly weary by mid-afternoon and retreated to the hammock for some much-needed relief from the summer heat, the steep, rocky trail and the bugs. It was impossible to get far off the trail and I set up only a few feet away. However, I snoozed soundly without disturbing anyone. In fact, I was so well camouflaged that other hikers passed without even noticing my hammock! Refreshed and leaving no trace of my presence, I was back on the trail an hour later.

Make your own hammock and you, too, can soon be enjoying superior sleep and rest in the wilderness!

You'll love a camping hammock
It's comfort fit for a king!

Chapter 2
The Convenience of
Hammock Camping

It's true--hammock campers have millions more places to set up than tent campers! Imagine the freedom and security of knowing you are carrying such a versatile and flexible shelter! This chapter should give you plenty of ideas.

In fact, deciding where to camp while on an outing can be safely postponed until it's actually time to make camp each night. Since set up takes only a few minutes, you can devote more of your day to whatever activity brought you outside in the first place. Imagine hiking, fishing, canoeing, rock climbing, etc. until dark or even later before making camp, knowing you will not be spending precious daylight hours searching for a suitable tent site in unfamiliar terrain.

On a recent seven-month hike on the Appalachian Trail, my hammock relieved me of the usual worry of finding nightly campsites and allowed me to hike many more miles each day. While my fellow hikers, unsure of available campsites ahead, often quit early at a known tent site, I hiked on with the knowledge I could easily make camp anywhere only moments after deciding to do so! In more than one case, while everyone else stopped early due to developing bad weather, I was able to continue hiking, stopping to make camp only at the last moments before the storm hit!

Avoiding Crowds

Appalachian Trail, Great Smoky Mountains National Park, NC
Mar 24, 2000

A dozen hikers have already been turned back. Camping in the park is restricted to only the established campsites and only one campsite on the AT is accessible by an afternoon hike from here. Since that campsite is already overcrowded, park rangers are not allowing campers without reservations, including AT hikers, to enter the park after 1:00 pm each day. Much to the envy of the frustrated hikers being held back, I am allowed to enter the park since my hammock allows me to use the campsite without the need for the limited space in the shelter or on the ground. The bewildered hikers watch as the ranger waves me on and I walk across the bridge. Although the site is crowded, I easily stay out of the way by setting up in the trees nearby.

Appalachian Trail, Ramrock Mtn., GA
Nov 11, 2001

The Veterans' Day weekend has brought out lots of campers. All of the numerous campsites along the trail were taken by mid-afternoon. I hiked on, intending to make camp long after dark. However, about dark, a friendly camping family invited me to dinner and we spent the next two hours eating and talking about the trail. When I got up to leave, they were shocked that I would hike on in the dark knowing that no campsites would be available. Although I explained the great advantage of my hammock system, they were still doubtful. While I easily found a suitable and comfortable spot for my hammock, I can't help but wonder that they must think I am crazy.

Mountains

Numerous times my hammock has been pitched on a high mountain site otherwise unsuited for tents or tarps. In such places I've had exclusive access to spectacular vistas, dramatic sunsets, the full moon flooding the forest and distant mountains, and colorful sunrises too numerous to mention. At these times, I feel especially close to nature and it seems as if the entire world is there just for my enjoyment.

Hammock on Rock Cliff

However, steep forested mountain slopes are one of my favorite stealth campsites. Many times I've pitched my hammock on slopes almost too steep to walk on! At times, the ground is so steep that my pack or gear cannot be left unattended or they will roll to the bottom! However, once inside my hammock, with my pack safely hanging below, I'm snug and comfortable!

Such sites are special because of their isolation, widespread availability, easy access, great views and the protection they provide from cold winds. By choosing these sites, I can be assured that I am not adding to the overuse of the more popular tent campsites in the backcountry. At the same time, my use of the site leaves no adverse impact and there is little chance the site will be used again before it recovers (see Chapter 4, "Hammock Camping Is Environmentally Friendly").

At other times, I avoid mountain sites that are exposed to cold wind. Many times I seek shelter from the wind behind steep ridges, occasionally leaving my fellow campers to suffer at more exposed tent sites on the ridge tops.

Hammock on Steep Slope

Hammocks on the Coast

Once in Florida and several times on the rocky coast of British Columbia, I pitched my hammock at water's edge at low tide and watched high tide flood in under me! Imagine the excitement as I watched the nighttime phosphorescence in the water immediately below me while staying snug and dry in my hammock!

Bears

Other times I've avoided bears by setting up in boulder fields, on rock cliffs, and on small isolated coastal islands in Alaska! Yes, I've actually set up my hammock between boulders and on rugged rock cliffs without trees!

Avoiding Bears

Admiralty Island, AK
Jul 1, 1989

True to its reputation as having the densest Brown Bear population in the world, Admiralty Island has not disappointed me; I saw 4 Browns while searching for a campsite today! The 12 1/2 mile crossing of Frederick Sound went better than expected. However, the sudden and fortunate mild weather brought dense fog and I had to paddle by compass most of the way. The only sound in the fog was the blowing of Humpback whales! I'm sleeping tonight in my hammock high in the treetops at the back of the beach. My food is also up here with me. Although there are lots of tracks and scat on the beach, no bears have showed up since I landed. I feel safe and all is well.

Angry eagles, which apparently don't like me in their trees, awaken me early the next morning. As the sun rises, I lounge in the hammock listening and watching Humpbacks feeding along the kelp line just 50 feet away!

Icy Strait, AK
Jul 7, 1989

I continue to see bear signs on every beach along the shore; no safe place to camp. Therefore, tonight I am on a small rocky island in Icy Strait; I hope this is far from normal bear habitat. There are no flat spots for my tent, so my hammock is strung low between several large rocks. The kayak is hauled out on the rocks above high tide. Strong headwinds and angry waves stopped me early today. Am spending the afternoon lying in my hammock, watching the waters of Icy Strait and the glacier-capped mountains in the distance. Orcas (killer whales), seals, eagles, and kittiwakes keep me entertained. I hear Humpbacks but cannot see them. No bears disturb my camp.   continued

Avoiding Bears (Cont'd.)

Queen Inlet, Glacier Bay, AK
Jul 23, 1989

After 5 days paddling among icebergs from calving tidewater glaciers, I've found a snug campsite in a boulder field at the base of a large cliff. Accessible only from the water, I'm safe from bears and protected from the strong afternoon winds. While many other campers are having nightly, and even daily, bear encounters, I feel perfectly safe here. My hammock is strung between a large breakdown boulder and the cliff itself. My kayak lies beneath the hammock. Although safe, I lie awake most of the night listening to the thunderous sounds of breeching Humpback whales as they feed nearby! These never-ending noises echo repeatedly throughout the rocky fiord. This may be one of the most memorable nights I'll ever spend in the wilderness.

Appalachian Trail, Kittatinny Mtn., NJ
Apr 29, 2001

My hiking partner prefers sleeping in the numerous shelters along the trail, so once again I've set up my hammock outside a shelter and he is set up inside. We both retired early after dinner and I was writing in my journal when the bear showed up. Ignoring me, the bear went straight for the shelter, where he had apparently found easy food before. Thankfully, we had already put all of our food in the metal bear box provided near the shelter. Mr. Bear jumped up into the shelter and, as my very frightened partner later told me, proceeded to sniff him from head to foot! Imagine opening your eyes and seeing a large Black Bear only an inch from your face! Not finding any food in the shelter, Mr. Bear jumped down, tried unsuccessfully to open the bear box, and then left. Although watching me in the hammock, he never came my way. The next day my partner placed an order for a hammock, which we picked up a few days later. That was the last time he ever stayed at a trail shelter!

The hammock allowed me to avoid active bear habitat and safely set up far from high-risk areas. More than once, I've used rock climbing ropes and gear to raise my hammock high in the trees out of the reach of bears.

Snakes

In the jungles of South America, we pitched our hammocks in trees to avoid the many dangerous snakes that prowl the ground at night. But snakes are also a worry elsewhere.

Avoiding Snakes

Little Inini River, French Guiana, South America
Feb 8, 1996

The storm hit suddenly and violently; it drove us off the river. Our Amazonian guide mysteriously maneuvered our dugout into the thick brush along the side of the river. Suddenly we touched land; how he found land in that flooded swamp and pouring deluge I will never know, since we had seen nothing but water for the past 10 hours. Safe from certain river drowning, we were now faced with another problem: how to set up camp to wait out the storm. Everything was soaked; even the ground was mostly mud. Within minutes, our guide had cut tree branches and was constructing sturdy supports over which we hung a large tarp. Next we strung our hammocks beneath the tarp and were soon lounging away as the storm raged around us. Getting my feet out of that mud never felt so good.

During the night, I got up to relieve myself and was surprised when our guide began yelling his disapproval. Grabbing my flashlight, I saw 2 snakes on the ground beneath our tarp! Hopping back into my hammock, I decided to wait 'til daylight before trying that again.

Almost every year I hear new stories about campers who found a snake in their sleeping bag. Sure enough, last year on the Appalachian Trail, I learned of a tarp camper who woke up one morning and found a snake by his feet at the bottom of his sleeping bag! Use a hammock to avoid these unnerving encounters.

Now that I carry a hammock all the time, I no longer worry about ground critters such as snakes, spiders, ticks, ants, or slugs. You, too, can say goodbye forever to these creepy crawlers by switching to a hammock.

Avoiding Bugs

Cloud Pond, Barren Mtn., ME
Jun 26, 2001

A long hard day on the trail made even more difficult by temps in the mid 90's! Black flies are extremely bad here at the campsite and everyone retreats to tents to lick their wounds; most skip cooking dinner since it means being exposed to the biting devils. I set up my hammock over large rocks near the lakeshore where warm wind keeps the little bastards away--my site is bug free! People watch me from their tents as I cook dinner and lounge in the hammock without the bug net.

Other Animals

Mice, which are a common concern at established campsites, are not a problem for the hammock camper in a stealth site off the beaten path. I simply hang my pack, including my food, from the hammock strap so that it is within easy reach and does not touch the ground. Although animals often visit my hammock site, they are not accustomed to finding people food there and never bother mine. I've often had rabbits, foxes, porcupines, raccoons, squirrels, chipmunks and others at my campsites without incident. Once a raccoon repeatedly passed beneath my hammock unaware of my food or me until I reached down and patted him on the back!

Rain

The large rain canopy provides ample protection and makes an unbeatable stand-up shelter for gentle rainy weather. There is plenty of room under the canopy for the hammock as well as for me. Being able to stand while doing camp chores such as changing clothes, loading/unloading the pack, or cooking dinner is a definite benefit not found in similar-weight tents.

Stand-up Shelter

The large canopy also facilitates making and breaking camp in the rain. On a long rainy day recently in Maine, I stopped to make camp several hours after dark. It was still raining hard and there had been nothing but rocks, trees and mud for miles. I found a beautiful spot beside a large lake; boulders covered the ground and no one had ever camped there before (and probably never will again). The rain canopy went up first. Since it was carried in an outside pocket, there was no need to open the pack and expose its contents to the pouring rain. Moments later I had a large protected shelter under which I then opened the pack and extracted the hammock. Only after the hammock was hung beneath the canopy did I remove my rain gear and finish making camp. In this manner, my gear was not exposed to the rain while I was setting up camp! Breaking camp in the rain is simply the reverse; the pack is loaded and rain gear donned before the canopy is taken down. All of this is done standing up! Anyone who has ever experienced making or breaking camp in the rain with a small tent or tarp on the ground can easily appreciate the simplicity and convenience of my hammock system!

Once I was forced off a high mountain ridge by an unexpected violent thunderstorm. The storm hit fast and the lightning was intense. I immediately took refuge by descending the rugged side of the ridge. Upon reaching a safe distance below the top, I set up my canopy and hammock to wait out the storm. The slope was extremely steep, but suitable trees were easily found. However, it was the next day before the storm abated and I could safely return to the summit and continue on my way. Without the hammock, I would have had to hike many miles on the exposed ridge during the storm in order to find a suitable camping spot. With the hammock, I was able to quickly find protection and actually enjoyed the storm while safely out of harm's way.

On another occasion, I set up my hammock close to the ground during an evening rainstorm and was able to cook dinner while lying down! Yes, I can be lazy. And why not? We're supposed to enjoy the wilderness, right?

When necessary, the rain canopy can be lowered as much as needed for complete protection from the elements (see following photographs).

Fair Weather Setup

Note that the extra-wide sides of the rain canopy can be lowered below the level of the hammock for complete rain protection

Stormy Weather Setup

Avoiding Rain

Appalachian Trail, Dana Hill, VT
Aug 9, 2001

This summer heat is getting brutal; probably over 100 again today. I've set up my hammock in trees well off the trail; no need to put up the tarp since it hasn't rained in weeks. Just at dark, all Hell breaks loose; high winds and blinding flashes announce the arrival of a thunderstorm! I get the tarp up only moments before the rain hits. Returning to my hammock, I'm soon back to sleep. Oh how satisfying it is to fall asleep listening to a raging storm, all the while knowing I'm snug and safe.

Appalachian Trail, NY
Aug 28, 2001

Another hot humid day, just like all of August has been. I fixed dinner in the mid-afternoon heat planning to hike the rest of the day and well into the night. Resumed hiking in bright sunshine at 4:40 pm; but was stopped thirty minutes later by a violent thunderstorm. Quickly set up hammock and canopy to wait out the storm. Resumed hiking at 6:30; stopped two hours after dark at 11:00.

Use on the Ground

My hammock system can be used on the ground when the need arises. Maybe I want to stay with friends who are tent camping in an area without suitable trees, or I'm in a treeless area, or temperatures unexpectedly drop below my comfort level. My hammock camping system is easily adapted for use on the ground. The hammock and bug net now serve as a bivy sack for the sleeping bag and the canopy is pitched overhead as a tarp using hiking poles as support. Sturdy sticks, generally easily found on the forest floor, can be substituted for the hiking poles. The canopy's eight-by-ten foot size is more than sufficient for a snug and dry ground shelter. The sleep pad, used as bottom insulation in the hanging hammock, now becomes cushioning for my bed on the ground.

Tarp Setup on Ground

The only additional item needed for ground use is a lightweight ground cloth. Since it is seldom used, my ground cloth is a 2.7 ounce four-by-ten foot piece of clear plastic (1 mil thick painters' drop cloth available at most hardware stores). Yes, it is fragile, but it functions well and can easily be replaced if damaged. Note that this ground cloth must be carried throughout the trip, thus it is also available for use as backup rain protection for the tree-hanging hammock. Although I have yet to use the ground cloth for rain protection, I have used it as a vapor barrier around the hammock as described in Chapter 3, "How To Stay Warm".

Rain Canopy

It is generally best to pitch the rain canopy longitudinally, or 'A' frame-like, between the tree supports above the hammock. However, it can be pitched diagonally with opposite corners attached to the trees above the hammock. Diagonal set up is faster since only four tie-outs are needed, as opposed to the six tie-outs needed for the longitudinal set up. However, diagonal set up offers less rain and wind protection.

I've used the diagonal set up for no-wind light drizzle with no potential for worsening weather. However, when the weather turns severe, I use the longitudinal set up for far more protection and peace of mind. Two extra pull-tabs on each side of the canopy can be used to attach additional guidelines if necessary in very strong winds. I generally avoid exposure to wind by camping on the protected side of hills or ridges, but if this is not possible it is nice to know I can use the extra side pull-tabs to prevent the wild flapping of the tarp that can occur in high winds.

At most stealth sites, the tarp guidelines can conveniently be tied out to trees, branches, brush, or even roots or rocks on the ground. If needed, sturdy dead sticks, often easily found on the forest floor, serve as stakes. Simply push them into the soft ground or place them behind rocks or roots. On most long trips in unfamiliar country, I carry six small tent stakes for potential set up, either hanging between trees or on the ground, where sticks are not available or are impractical.

Rain Canopy Guidelines

The cord chosen for the guidelines on the rain canopy is critical since the wrong cord can cause major headaches and can even be dangerous. Most lightweight limp cords are unsuitable; they will tangle unmercifully in brush, weeds, grasses and tree limbs. Limp cord even tangles badly with itself.

There are 60 feet of guidelines on my tarp; these long lengths are needed to allow the tarp to be pitched over the hanging hammock or on the ground. Imagine spending ten minutes or more untangling these lines every time you set up the trap. It can take more time than setting up the tarp and hammock in the first place. Nothing is more frustrating than having to untangle lines in the rain or cold weather.

Using a stiff cord, such as the solid-core, nylon-sheath cord recommended in Chapter 6, "How To Make Your Own Hammock," can greatly reduce tangle problems.

New Freedom

The newfound freedom of the hammock camper is mesmerizing and the list of suitable stealth campsites in the wilderness is long and exciting. The possible wilderness sites tempting the hammock camper are endless. But with your new freedom comes new responsibilities (see Chapter 4, "Hammock Camping Is Environmentally Friendly").

Take a hammock on your next wilderness trip and experience the wonder of Nature all over again!

64 - Hammock Camping

I absolutely love this hammock. It is a lot faster to set up and take down than my tent and of course I do not have to look for a flat smooth surface to set it up on. I was worried in the Shenandoah's when there were high winds accompanied by hail the size of marbles, but I stayed dry. That same night, a hiker using a hammock with a smaller rain canopy retreated to the shelter from the wind driven rain.

Chris Stevens, 2002 hiking the East Continental Trail with a Speer Hammock

Chapter 3
How To Stay Warm

Rapid heat loss from the bottom of a hammock, one of its greatest advantages in hot humid weather, quickly becomes uncomfortable as the temperatures drop below about 75°F. For cooler temperatures, the hammock user, especially the overnight sleeper, requires bottom insulation for comfort. Items already in the wilderness traveler's pack, such as extra clothes, a sleeping bag and/or a sleep pad can usually provide the needed insulation. As temperatures drop even more however, additional measures are necessary. This chapter explores the options and suggests some innovative solutions.

Sleeping bags alone are often inadequate since their insulation is compressed flat beneath the hammock user, providing little protection from bottom heat loss. Adding a thicker and often unacceptably heavier sleeping bag doesn't always work well either. I've often been sweaty hot on top yet uncomfortably cold on the bottom until I learned to control the total heat loss.

Preventing Heat Loss

Body heat loss is a complicated interaction involving conduction, convection, radiation, evaporation and respiration. For maximum comfort, managing heat loss also means managing body moisture (respiration and perspiration). No wonder trying to stay warm is such a battle! But there is hope (see diagram below).

An informative discussion on insulation and staying warm in the outdoors can be found on the Internet at: **www.3m.com.market/consumer/thinsulate/warmtips1.html**. Be sure to also check the other information links at this web site.

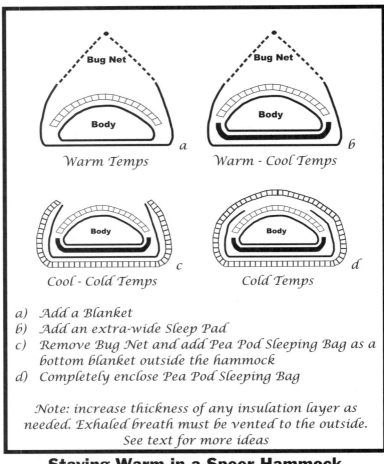

Warm Temps   *a*

Warm - Cool Temps   *b*

Cool - Cold Temps   *c*

Cold Temps   *d*

a) *Add a Blanket*
b) *Add an extra-wide Sleep Pad*
c) *Remove Bug Net and add Pea Pod Sleeping Bag as a bottom blanket outside the hammock*
d) *Completely enclose Pea Pod Sleeping Bag*

Note: increase thickness of any insulation layer as needed. Exhaled breath must be vented to the outside. See text for more ideas

Staying Warm in a Speer Hammock

The following simple examples should help illustrate the battles of staying warm. Conductive heat transfer occurs between objects in contact, such as warm skin and cold air, or a finger and a hot stove. Convective heat transfer involves motion, such as air currents that carry heat away. Radiant heat refers to the transfer of heat through space, such as the sun radiating heat to the earth. Evaporative heat transfer involves the heat required to evaporate body moisture from our skin (insensible perspiration). Lastly, respiration heat is lost through our expelled breath.

One scientific study found that the human body at rest losses 76% of its' heat due to conduction, convection and radiation; the remaining 24% is lost through evaporation, insensible perspiration and respiration.

The good news is that modern hi-tech materials give us a lot of ammunition to work with. Thick insulation with tiny dead-air spaces used in sleeping bags and sleep pads, and thick clothing such as fleece or pile are effective against conductive and convective heat loss. Tight-weave, wind-proof and reflective fabrics can greatly reduce convective and radiant heat loss, but often do so at the cost of trapping unwanted condensation. Evaporative heat loss can be the most difficult to tackle. It can however, be addressed by the use of vapor barriers between the skin and the insulation (but never around the face).

Heat loss due to respiration (expelled warm breath) can be reduced by use of the bug net to help hold the warm air near the body. Yes, bug netting is a vapor barrier, just not a very good one. It is good enough, though, that it should be vented as necessary to prevent the buildup of excessive humidity. Exhaling inside a sleeping bag should be avoided since it adds unwanted water moisture to the insulation.

Fabric color, although seldom considered in sleeping bag manufacture, also affects radiant heat transfer. Everyone has noticed that a black or dark-colored shirt "absorbs" more of the sun's radiant heat on a sunny day than a white or light-colored shirt. The dark fabric simply transfers much of the sun's radiant heat to your skin, while the light fabric reflects much of it back toward the source, which is the sun itself. Since you are the heat source in a sleeping bag, using light-colored fabrics around you will reflect more of the heat back to you while dark fabrics would allow more of it to escape. This is probably the real reason Poplar Bears are white!

Highly reflective aluminized fabrics can work even better since they can reflect as much as 97% of the radiant heat back to the source! See more on these unique fabrics below.

Ground sleepers benefit greatly from the reduction in heat loss (conductive, convective and radiant) provided by the ground itself. We aerial sleepers are immersed in the heat-robbing air and need extra help. But using heavier gear is not always the best answer! The remainder of this chapter offers numerous successful solutions for the hammock sleeper.

Vapor Proof Treatments

In an earlier chapter, I mentioned the use of spray-on vapor-proof treatments to seal the bottom hammock fabric against the entry of cold air (to reduce convective heat loss). This is often my first line of defense in the battle to stay warm as the seasonal temperatures drop. Waterproof or windproof treatments work equally well. They are readily available and easily applied without adding any significant weight to the hammock. The usual silicone or durable-water-resistant (DWR) treatments come in convenient spray cans and can be purchased at outdoors stores or sporting goods departments of large variety retailers. In 2002, a 10.5-

ounce can of Silicone Water-Guard cost about $3 at Wal-Mart. It is sufficient for two applications; allow the fabric to dry between sprayings. Two of these silicone treatments add about 0.6 ounce to an eight-by-five foot hammock.

Although silicone treatments are less expensive and may be more vapor proof than DWR treatments, they may also be harder to remove by washing as described earlier; try multiple washings with detergent and fabric softener. Many hammock fabrics come with original DWR treatments and may not need additional treatments until they have undergone multiple washings.

Sealing the fabric in this way for winter use effectively blocks some cold outside air from passing through the hammock fabric. It also helps keep the warm air inside. This helps stop the convective heat loss due to moving air (i.e., wind) through the bottom fabric. Once warm temperatures return, the vapor-proof treatments can be removed to allow cooling and condensation-preventing air to circulate once again.

Sealing the bottom fabric however, does not stop the equally serious conductive heat loss due to contact with cold air. In other words, a warm body in the hammock will continue to rapidly lose bottom heat unless sufficient insulation separates the camper from the cold outside air. A sleeping bag works fine by providing insulation on top, but it is compressed by the weight of the hammock user and gives practically no insulation on the bottom. Non-crushable sleep pads however, can effectively provide the needed insulation.

How Much Insulation is Needed?

How much insulation is needed at any given time? This, of course, depends on many variables, such as the outside temperature, your tendency to sleep hot or cold, your sleeping bag's insulation, your sleep pad's thickness, the clothes you wear, the amount of air passing through the hammock fabric, the amount of wind reaching the hammock, etc. The following table is based on my comfort in no-wind conditions, but should give you some guidelines.

Sleeping Bags and Sleep Pads Inside a Hammock

>75°F	Thin cotton sheet & no sleeping pad
70-75°F	48°-rated sleeping bag & no pad
60-70°F	48°-rated sleeping bag & 1/4" pad
50-60°F	38°-rated sleeping bag & 1/4" pad
40-50°F	25°-rated sleeping bag & 1/2" pad
30-40°F	25°-rated sleeping bag & 1" pad
20-30°F	15°-rated sleeping bag & 2" pad
10-20°F	0°-rated sleeping bag & 2" pad

While these figures might at first seem like too much insulation, you should remember that hammocks are completely surrounded by air, which is often colder than the ground. In addition, I tend to sleep cold and may need more insulation than you do.

Of course, these are only suggestions and there are no hard and fast rules here. There are many possible sleeping bag/sleep pad combinations and only you can judge which one is right for you. The general idea is to choose a sleeping bag to keep you warm on the top and choose a sleep pad to keep you warm on the bottom. Later in this chapter you will find an alternate way to use a sleeping bag around the occupied hammock for even more warmth.

Sleeping Bag

Wearing a sleeping bag inside a hammock takes some getting used to. It can be confining and difficult to get into or out of. It is easier to use the unzipped bag as a blanket over you with your feet inserted into the foot end. This is more comfortable since it allows greater freedom to move around inside the hammock. Use a sleep pad for bottom insulation.

As temperatures drop however, there comes a point where it is warmer to get inside the sleeping bag while also using the sleep pad.

Cold Wind

Cold wind will greatly change the insulation suggestions given above. Remember that the hammock camper already suffers from rapid heat loss on the bottom, and cold wind will greatly aggravate this problem. If cold wind is encountered or expected, the above suggestions should be appropriately modified. This generally means that you should move down at least one gear level in the table to maintain comfort.

Sleeping Pads

Regular outdoor sleep pads work fine, although they may not be wide enough (see below). You can choose from closed-cell foam pads or open-cell foam-filled inflatable pads, increasing the thickness to suit the need. I can generally get by with a single pad for weeks to months at a time, before changing temperatures force me to switch.

Of course, not all sleeping pads are equally suitable for hammocks. Pads at least 24 inches wide are preferable since the hammock wraps around the body and side protection is needed; some folks probably will want even wider pads. Unfortunately, most closed-cell foam pads are sold in widths less than 24 inches.

Hammock with Sleep Pad

Closed-cell foam pads are readily available from most outdoor and sporting goods stores. They vary from 1/4 to 3/4 inch thick and generally are 20 inches wide and 72 inches long. All models can be used in hammocks. Of course, greater warmth comes at the expense of greater weight. Models with deep air-pocket features, such as the Z-Rest and Ridge Rest pads of Cascades Designs, Inc., effectively create greater thickness, and thus greater warmth, than solid pads of the same weight.

Unfortunately, most adults will find that the standard 20-inch widths of these pads are minimal as mentioned above. More suitable 24-inch wide pads include the inexpensive Coleman Ultralight Camp Pad sold by various sporting-goods and general retailers or the Ozark Trail Egg Crate Camping pad sold by Wal-Mart. The Ozark Trail pad is a wise choice since it is also "grippy" and does not slide around inside a hammock like many other pads.

Even wider pads provide better protection; however these are harder to find. Thin closed-cell foam pads up to 60 inches wide can be purchased at some fabric stores; mail-order sources include Quest Outfitters, Outdoor Wilderness Fabrics, The Rain Shed, Inc., and Seattle Fabrics, Inc. Since pads greater than 40 inches wide buckle excessively and create uncomfortable folds, these wide pads can easily be trimmed to suitable widths with large scissors. One-forth-inch thick pads up to 40 inches wide can be ordered from Speer Hammocks, Inc. Wide Reflectix pads are also a wise choice and are discussed in the following section.

For warm summer use, you can save weight and bulk by using scissors to shorten any closed-cell foam pad since insulation below the knees is generally not needed. Trimming the square corners of wide or full-length foam pads provides a better fit in the curved world of a hammock (see diagram).

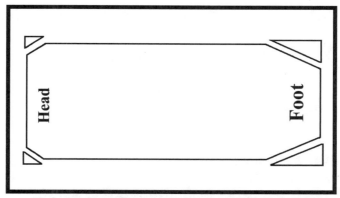

Trimming Foam Pad for Better Fit

Closed-cell foam pads 1/4" X 30" X 72" weigh about 11 ounces and make excellent hammock liners for warm or moderate temperatures. For cold temperatures, combining a thin, wide liner pad with a thicker, but narrower, three-quarter-length foam or inflatable pad may provide all the bottom insulation needed.

Self-inflatable pads offer greater thickness and may offer greater insulating warmth than closed-cell foam pads. Pads filled with open-cell foam, which create millions of tiny air pockets that reduce conductive and convective heat loss may be a wise choice. Unfortunately, they can add considerable weight.

Self-inflatable pads are readily available from most outdoors and sporting goods stores. They vary in thickness from 3/4 inch to 3 inches and are generally 22 inches wide and 72 inches long; the thicker ones may be considerably wider. They all work well in hammocks and range from one to seven pounds. Some popular brands include those produced by Slumberjack, Stearns and Artiach, as well as the Therm-A-Rest line by Cascade Designs. Inflatable pads with non-skid surfaces are well suited for hammocks.

Inflatable pads filled with down offer significantly more insulating thickness with less weight than foam-filled pads. A three-inch thick pad weighing 1.5 pounds is available from Stephenson's Warmlite.

See the information box for sleep pad manufacturers and suppliers.

Radiant Heat Pads

Some hammock campers successfully keep warm using innovative sleep pads that have high heat-reflective surfaces--such as aluminum-covered automobile windshield sunscreens! Radiant heat reflectors do work!

These sunscreen/sleep pads are commonly made from Reflectix, which is a five-sixteenth-inch-thick laminate of plastic bubble wrap sandwiched between layers of aluminum foil. The foil may reflect as much as

Sources for Sleep Pads

Casa Artiach, S.A.
C./ Trabajo, 8
50008 Zaragoza. Espana
34-976-421-100
Email: info@artiach.com

Cascade Designs, Inc.
4000 First Ave. S
Seattle, WA 98134
800-531-9531
www.cascadedesigns.com
Email: consumer@cascadedesigns.com

The Coleman Co., Inc.
3600 N. Hydraulic
Wichita, KS 67219
800-835-3278
www.coleman.com
Email: consumerservice@coleman.com

High Country Outdoor Products
800-304-4442
www.highcop.com

Quest Outfitters
4919 Hubner
Sarasota, FL 34241
800-359-6931
www.questoutfitters.com
Email: questoutfitters@home.com

The Rain Shed, Inc.
707 NW 11th
Corvallis, OR 97330
541-753-8900

Reflectix, Inc.
#1 School Street
PO Box 108
Markleville, IN 46056
800-879-3645
www.reflectixinc.com
Email: customerservice@reflectixinc.com

continued

Sources for Sleep Pads (Cont'd.)

Seattle Fabrics, Inc.
8702 Aurora Ave. N
Seattle, WA 98103
206-525-0670
www.seattlefabrics.com

Slumberjack Products
PO Box 7048-A
Saint Louis, MO 63177
800-233-6283
www.slumberjack.com
Email: info@slumberjack.com

Speer Hammocks, Inc.
34 Clear Creek Road
Marion, NC 28752-6407
828-724-4444
www.speerhammocks.com
Email: info@speerhammocks.com

Stearns, Inc.
1100 Stearns Drive
Sauk Rapids, MN 56397
800-333-1179
www.stearnsinc.com
Email: stearns@stearnsnet.com

Stephenson's Warmlite
22 Hook Road
Gilford, NH 03246-6745
603-293-8526
www.warmlite.com
Email: inquires@warmlite.com

Wal-Mart Stores, Inc.
702 SW 8th Street
Bentonville, AR 72716
800-925-6278
www.walmart.com

97% of the radiant heat that otherwise would be lost from the bottom of a hammock!

In addition to the radiant-heat reflectors in Reflectix, the dead-air space in the bubble wrap provides insulation that reduces conductive heat loss. Reflectix in widths of 24 or 48 inches can be purchased at some home improvement stores; it can easily be trimmed with scissors. The finished windshield sunscreens can be purchased at most automotive supply stores. Sleep pads made from Reflectix up to 40 inches wide can also be purchased from Speer Hammocks, Inc. (see the information box).

Radiant Reflector Sleep Pad

Reflectix pads may safely be substituted for foam or inflatable pads in many cases or they may be used in combination for greater warmth. Reflectix pads 5/16" X 30" X 72" weigh about 12 ounces and make effective liners for hammocks since they provide excellent side and bottom protection. The square corners should be trimmed as mentioned above for foam pads.

Unfortunately, Reflectix pads are fragile and easily damaged, especially if used on the rough ground. In hammocks, they may function properly only a few weeks and thus are best suited for short cold-weather trips. While less heat efficient, similarly sized closed-cell foam pads are better suited for longer wilderness trips.

Since it also reduces the escape of body vapor, using a wide full-length pad inside a hammock may cause excessive condensation in your sleeping bag. Removing the bug net, using a sleeping bag with breathable fabrics and air-drying it as much as possible each day may alleviate this problem.

When colder temperatures result in greater conductive heat loss, fold thin pads double, switch to thicker foam or inflatable pads, or use a combination of pads, such as a thirty-inch wide full length pad (1/4" foam or 5/16" Reflectix) and a thicker three-quarter length foam or inflatable pad. Again, there are many possible choices in the battle for warmth.

A Better Way to Warmth

The wilderness traveler concerned with pack weight and bulk must carefully judge which sleeping bag/pad combination is right for him/her. Rather than carrying the heavier pads, I've found some other cold-weather techniques that work well and save weight. One is to hide from the wind by setting up on the lee side of a hill or ridge; another is to rig my sleeping bag completely around the hammock!

Hide from the Wind

I've already mentioned the concept of avoiding the wind by camping in wind-protected spots. It's worth repeating again. This technique is extremely effective and is almost always available to the hammock camper. All you need to do is search for suitable trees or rocks on the wind-sheltered sides of ridges, hills, mountains, or even rock cliffs. Generally you only need to be slightly below the top to get complete protection; in fact, being too far below the top can put you back in the windy zone.

Hide from the Wind

I have often hung my hammock only a few feet vertically below a ridgeline or hilltop and listened all night to hurricane-force winds in the treetops directly above me, while I enjoyed perfectly calm conditions! It's as if I am in a vacuum while the rest of the world around me is being blown apart. Tent or tarp campers are seldom lucky enough to be able to use sites like these (see the information boxes for related stories).

Sleeping Bag Around the Hammock

Moving your sleeping bag to the outside of the hammock offers the greatest possible increase in warmth and comfort without adding any extra weight.

It is possible to increase a hammock's warmth by adding such things as heavier fabrics or insulation. In the battle for warmth however, it's probably better to add any required extra weight to the sleeping bag and/or sleep pad, which have multiple uses, rather than to the hammock itself, which has limited uses. For instance, the sleeping bag and sleep pad will sometimes be used without the hammock, but the hammock is seldom used without the sleeping bag or sleep pad. It is therefore wiser to add any required new weight to the sleeping bag or sleep pad.

Avoiding Wind

Appalachian Trail, Peter's Mountain, PA
Apr 18, 2001

Expecting 25-30^{0}F tonight; unusual spring cold snap with snow flurries. Strong northwest winds make for brutal hiking along the ridge top; camping on the flat ridge top is suicidal. I've set up my hammock on the steep east side of the ridge, about 150 feet vertically below the ridge top. Although cold, at least I am out of the wind. Three other hikers are not so lucky, they are forced to use the hiking shelter on the ridge top, which is directly in the path of the cold wind.

Mount Mitchell, Black Mountains, NC
Jan 31, 1999

The Black Mountains, the highest mountain range in the eastern US, catch the blunt of each winter storm and focus ferocious winds around its peaks. Tonight I've pitched my hammock beneath a small rock cliff well below the mountain crest. The wind is screaming over the ridge, but I am secure in my protected nest. About 20 others have set up camp in the beautiful grassy meadow nearby, but they are exposed to the cold wind. Individual blasts of wind roar down the mountainside, sounding like fast-moving freight trains as they come toward me only to be deflected at the last moment by the rock cliff above me. It's going to be cold tonight, as low as 10^0. Sure glad I brought two sleeping bags!

The wind is still blowing the next morning and breaking camp is a challenge in the bitter cold. One tent in the open meadow was actually blown away during the night when the camper got up to answer the call of nature! Many of the tenters stayed awake battling the wind all night, while I slept without a worry.

continued

Avoiding Wind (Cont'd.)

Appalachian Trail, Marble Spring Campsite, VA
Oct 1, 2001

Cold northwest wind is blowing strong tonight, so I've set up my hammock about 300' down the eastern ridge side. I'm completely out of the wind, while my hiking partner, restricted to the flat camping site on the ridge top, is exposed to the cold wind and suffers greatly in his bivy sack. The wind blows most of the night with near hurricane force.

Appalachian Trail, Mount Rodgers, VA
Oct 16, 2001

Cold windy day with snow flurries; expect 25-30^{0}F tonight. Three other hikers are sleeping in the trail shelter, but it faces the brutal cold wind and they will have an unpleasant night. I've set up my hammock behind a ridge and out of the wind. My water bottle is frozen by morning, but I slept warm.

Shortoff Mtn., Linville Gorge Wilderness Area, NC
Jan 18, 1999

Although I've set up near the edge of the mountain cliff, my hammock is out of the 50 mph winds that are blowing up the face of the cliff. Trees only a few feet from me are nearly torn apart by the winds, while I am in a near vacuum. Standing on the edge of the cliffs, I can actually extend my hand through an invisible wall that separates the calm air around me from the raging wind beyond; a true freak of nature! I entertain myself by tossing sticks over the cliff and watching them soar back over my head and then land behind me. I sleep securely while less than 20 feet away the wind is nearly tearing branches off the trees.

But remember that the bottom of a sleeping bag, even a cold-weather bag, is compressed flat inside a hammock and gives little to no insulating warmth there. The solution is to put the sleeping bag on the outside where it can provide insulation on the top as well as the bottom!

Pea Pod Bed

I use a unique sleeping bag made to fit around the hammock. I actually string the hammock through my sleeping bag! I call it my "Pea Pod Bed"; it keeps me as warm and snug as a bug in a rug!

Pea Pod Sleeping Bag Around Hammock

Yes, it does look funny; just like a sleeping bag floating in the air!

The Pea Pod Sleeping Bag has drawstring closures on both ends that allow it to fit symmetrically around the hammock. Full-length hook and loop fasteners give easy access and allow the sleeping bag to be placed completely around a previously set up hammock. Of course, the sleeping bag can be easily used by itself for those times when the hammock is not used.

The Pea Pod Sleeping Bag also doubles as a convenient robe for use in camp. Since it opens symmetrically at both ends, the bag easily converts to a super-warm robe and saves weight and bulk by eliminating the need for extra camp clothes.

Pea Pod Sleeping Bag
Worn as a Robe

A custom-made version of this bag can be ordered from Speer Hammocks, Inc. (see the information box).

Used alone or in combination with a light blanket and a thin extra-wide sleep pad, the Pea Pod Sleeping Bag makes a warm nest for most three-season camping. As temperatures drop, replacing the light blanket with increasingly warmer ones and adding another sleep pad (such as a thicker yet shorter and narrower pad) makes a sensible system for hammock warmth. See the rest of this chapter for even more ways to stay warm.

Unfortunately, the popular mummy-type sleeping bags that most people already have work poorly around a hammock. They are generally too constrictive in girth and their asymmetrical foot opening causes serious loss of useable length. While they can be used in an emergency, most people will find them uncomfortably restrictive and too short to keep their head and shoulders warm. Rectangular sleeping bags and zippered fleece liners may work fine. Try whatever sleeping bag you currently have and see if it works for you.

Source for Pea Pod
Sleeping Bags

Speer Hammocks Inc. offers the Pea Pod Sleeping Bag, which is custom made to fit around a hammock. It has full-length hook and loop fasteners and drawstring closures on both ends to accommodate the hammock. It is sized extra large to eliminate the loss of insulating loft caused by over crowding. It comes with breathable shells in a variety of sizes and insulating thickness. It can easily be worn as a robe, thus eliminating the need for extra camp clothes.

Speer Hammocks, Inc.
34 Clear Creek Road
Marion, NC 28752-6407
828-724-4444
www.speerhammocks.com
Email: info@speerhammocks.com

Still Need Sleep Pad

On short mild-weather trips that lack the need to sleep on the ground, it may be possible to use the hammock with The Pea Pod Sleeping Bag without any additional insulation. On long or fowl-weather trips however, the Pea Pod setup generally does not eliminate the need for a sleep pad. Remember the sleep pad is occasionally needed on the ground anyway when the hammock is not used; therefore, it probably still needs to be carried. If it has to be carried anyway, it should be used as part of a complete stay-warm system. The trick is to balance the weight of the sleeping bag and the sleep pad for the best overall advantage.

Dry leaves placed between the Pea Pod Sleeping Bag and the hammock make a highly efficient 'natural' insulation. Leaves are almost always available and can be used if your gear is not up to the task; just remember to return them to where you gathered them.

Note that the head is outside the sleeping bag so moisture-rich exhaled breath can escape
A clothes-filled stuff sack serves as a pillow and supports the head
Remember to keep your head well protected

Cold Weather Setup

Other Ways to Stay Warm

Don't forget, other ways to increase the warmth of any sleeping bag include eating well, drinking excess water, covering your head, wearing extra clothes, adding an over bag, adding an inner liner, or using inside vapor barriers. These additional methods are mentioned to make the point that you have an arsenal of choices for adding warmth to your sleeping bag. Unfortunately, adding an extra warm body is not recommended in a hammock designed for one person!

Eating nutritious and easily digested food provides calories that generate inner warmth. Your body is your only heat source and it needs proper fuel to function well.

At rest, our bodies produce this inner heat by consuming a whopping 50-calories/hour/square meter of body surface area! That adds up to a lot of calories consumed during a single night. Obviously eating no food or poor food means less body heat generated during the night. Eating just before going to bed and/or snacking during the night is very effective. To facilitate digestion and circulation, avoid dehydration by drinking **lots** of water both day and night.

As much as 70% of body heat is lost through the head, so be sure to keep it covered. If the head is cold, the body will actually shut down blood circulation (i.e., heating) to legs, feet, arms and hands in an effort to re-warm the head. A balaclava or hood makes an excellent head covering since they stay in place better than hats that are less secured.

Fleece fabrics are effective for warmth since they create insulating thickness by trapping air in millions of tiny pockets that do not collapse completely beneath the hammock sleeper. Adding fleece garments, liners, or blankets can greatly increase the warmth of a hammock sleeper in cold weather.

Vapor Barrier Fabrics

Properly used vapor barrier bags and sheets can effectively increase the warmth of any sleeping bag. However, the incorrect use of vapor barriers can dangerously decrease warmth, comfort and safety. All of the following options should be completely mastered before heading for the backcountry.

A vapor barrier (VB) bag can be used **inside** the sleeping bag for 10-15⁰ F added warmth. Some people however, find that such bags are uncomfortable. Thin long-john underwear can be worn to keep the VB fabric and any condensed moisture away from the skin. An informative discussion on cold-weather vapor barrier use can be found on the Internet at: **www.warmlite.com/vb.htm**.

A VB bag traps body vapor close to the skin and quickly raises the inside humidity to 100%; this then shuts down the body's excessive heat loss due to the evaporation of the always present insensible perspiration from the skin. Once no longer needed to evaporate this perspiration to water vapor, this heat stays in the body and slowly builds up warmth during the night.

Of course, using a VB bag also keeps body moisture, dirt and skin oils out of the sleeping bag, thus reducing the need to dry or wash it. Washing the VB bag is much easier than washing the sleeping bag.

Use of a full length VB bag with reflective light-colored fabrics can effectively reduce convective, radiant, and evaporative heat loss. This simple inexpensive and lightweight option is an excellent way to add warmth to a sleeping bag or hammock.

Rain suits or wind suits, which are generally present in every camper's pack anyway, can be worn inside a sleeping bag as makeshift VB bags.

For an extra-warm VB and radiant-heat reflector combination, you can use an aluminized Mylar sheet between the hammock and the Pea Pod Sleeping Bag. The Mylar sheet, such as one of the popular light-weight emergency or survival blankets available at most outdoor specialty stores, simply rests inside the sleeping bag where it blocks bottom air flow and keeps body moisture from getting into that portion of the bag's insulation that is beneath you.

Note however, that although adding great warmth, these VB sheets can result in excessive condensation of body moisture inside the hammock, which may wet the hammock fabric, you, and that portion of the sleeping bag over the top of you. Use of a VB sheet in this manner may only be appropriate in extreme drying conditions such as cool, windy, low-humidity weather since cold or high-humidity weather will almost surely cause excessive condensation. However, the proper use of VB sheets can greatly add warmth with very little increase in weight. Be sure to experiment at home before challenging the wilderness.

Any waterproof sheet, such as the ground sheet usually carried in the pack anyway for those times when the hammock is used as a bivy sack on the ground, can be substituted for the reflective Mylar sheet described above. Although slightly less efficient, a lightweight plastic ground sheet works well in certain conditions when used between the Pea Pod Sleeping Bag and the hanging hammock.

Avoid using any waterproof or near-waterproof fabric on the **outside** of your sleeping bag since it will trap body moisture inside the insulation. This includes avoiding use of plastic sheets, tarps, radiant reflectors such as aluminized films, and those waterproof-breathable fabrics that are currently popular in bivy sacks or over bags that fit around a sleeping bag. The breathable, DWR-treated, tight-weave fabrics usually found on good-quality sleeping bags should be sufficient to block cold wind (thus blocking conductive and convective heat loss) while not trapping excessive moisture inside.

Remember to vent your moisture-rich exhaled breath to the outside, not inside your sleeping bag. In below-freezing temperatures, exhaled breath trapped inside a bug-net-covered hammock may condense and freeze safely out of the way on the inside of the bug net. In near-freezing temperatures however, this condensation may not freeze, or may re-melt and drip back onto the sleeping bag. Prevent this by not using the bug net or occasionally venting it during the night. Getting up once or twice during the night to answer the call of nature may not create sufficient ventilation.

Vapor barrier bags or sheets **should never be used over the face** since they can block breathing and cause suffocation. Remember the infant deaths caused by thin plastic bags when they first became widely available? VB fabrics should cover the body only from the neck down.

Once again, there are many choices in the battle for warmth. If interested in VB fabrics, you should master their use on short, mild-weather outings before committing to long or cold-weather trips.

Some Hammocks Don't Work

Not all hammocks are suitable for my Pea Pod setup. Hammocks with permanently attached bug nets and ridgelines may not accommodate a sleeping bag on the outside. Hammocks with removable bug nets and bug net support lines are a better choice.

Now, if you go back to the temperature vs. sleeping bag/sleep pad table given earlier in this chapter, you will see that eating well, drinking water, hiding from the wind, wind proofing the fabrics, using VB fabrics, using wide and/or radiant heat pads and liners, and using the Pea Pod Sleeping Bag give you even more options for staying warm. For any given conditions, you may now be able to move up a gear level on the table and still be warm.

Only your experience using your gear can tell you what works best for you. Experiment before going into the wilderness. You should only use my suggestions here as guidelines. The good news is you can stay warm in a hammock with the same items you might normally be carrying anyway.

Extreme Cold Weather

For those interested in extreme cold weather use, there is hope. I leave it to you however, to expand on the concepts mentioned here. My only advice is that it's going to be much colder than you are accustomed to from sleeping on the ground. Be careful and have backup gear available, at least until you gain experience. And remember, when you get cold in your hammock, simply switch to sleeping on the ground, returning to the comfort of the hammock as soon as temperatures allow.

Both comfort and warmth are possible in a hammock!

Chapter 4
Hammock Camping Is Environmentally Friendly

Hammock camping offers some exciting environmental advantages, not the least of which is the potential to reduce the overuse so common at many backcountry campsites. Without harming trees, soil, or ground-cover plants, hammock use can be benign and offers a wise alternative to tents or tarps. Our forested backcountry can simply absorb hammock campers much more easily than it can ground campers.

Hammocks allow an easier way to follow the new wilderness ethics promoted by the Leave No Trace program. This worthy program strives to reduce our adverse impact on the environment through education, practice and example. All hammock campers are strongly urged to join and support the Leave No Trace organization (see the information box).

Overused Tent Sites
Everyone who has spent time in the wilderness has seen

the damage caused by the repeated use of tent sites. The choicest sites, even deep in the wilderness, are generally the most abused. All tent users, of course, search for the same thing: level ground free of brush and rocks. So much the better if the site offers scenic values and happens to be near a water source. Everyone wants to camp in the same place; there just simply aren't enough suitable sites. On many occasions I have watched in dismay the continuous parade of tent campers using a single site; as soon as one party packs up and departs, a new party takes its place.

One recent three-day holiday on a trail in north Georgia serves to make my point. By mid-afternoon of the first day, the best scenic campsites along a beautiful mountain ridge were occupied. Confident I could set up my hammock anywhere, I continued hiking but met dozens of arriving hikers who were desperately trying to find campsites before dark. Each frantically asked me if I had seen any unoccupied sites. The few available tent sites could not accommodate the large number of campers. Over the three days, each tent site was in constant use. It would take the ground at these sites several years of no further use just to recover from this single holiday! But the sites just keep getting used over and over again, year after year.

The bare ground at sites like these, surrounded by otherwise lush growth, attests to the damage of the tents and the many pounding feet. The soil at these places becomes so compacted that plants such as grasses can no longer sprout. Without ground cover, erosion can run rampant. At many heavily used sites, the ground becomes so compacted that tent stakes must be hammered in! And yet the tent users keep coming back to the same sites in ever increasing numbers.

Leave No Trace
Principles of Outdoor Ethics

1. Plan Ahead and Prepare
2. Travel and Camp on Durable Surface
3. Dispose of Waste Properly
4. Leave What You Find
5. Minimize Campfire Impacts
6. Respect Wildlife
7. Be Considerate of Other Visitors

Leave No Trace, Inc.
PO Box 997
Boulder, Co 80306
800-332-4100
www.LNT.org

See Appendix 4 for more information on the Leave No Trace principles of responsible outdoor use. Join and support this worthy organization. Above all, become a Leave No Trace camper yourself and set an example for others

Forest rangers and others responsible for managing and protecting our outdoor areas have few options to stop the campsite abuse. Shutting down a popular campsite for the tens of years necessary for the land to recover is seldom successful as tent users, with no suitable alternatives, soon return and ignore the posted restrictions.

As suggested by the Leave No Trace program, it may be best for the time being to allow these high-abuse tent campers to continue using the same sites anyway, to prevent spreading their damage to other areas of the wilderness. Once these tent campers learn, accept and follow the Leave No Trace principles, they can begin to safely wander beyond the overused campsites. By following the Leave No Trace principles now, the hammock camper can unobtrusively and harmlessly camp in more pristine areas. See the information box here and Appendix 4 for more on the Leave No Trace principles.

Hammocks are Better

Hammocks offer an obvious workable alternative to tent camping. Hammock campers can easily disperse into the forest far beyond the congested tent campsites. The vast number of suitable hammock campsites ensures that any single site is less likely to be used again before it recovers from the first use.

Often you can avoid crowds and still find unique campsites

Avoiding Crowds

But doesn't hammock camping also cause some damage? Of course, it can. However, if used conscientiously, the impact is as close to Leave No Trace camping as you can get. Generally the impact is only some ruffled leaves on the ground or some trampled grass. Often there is no visible impact at all. Most of the time, only a good bloodhound could ever find where you've camped!

But won't choice hammock sites become overused as increasing numbers of people switch to hammocks? Yes, unless we, the hammock campers, prevent it. Join Leave No Trace today and follow their outdoor-use principles.

Avoiding Crowded Campsites

Appalachian Trail, White Cap Mountain, ME
Jul 6, 2001

A summer cold front is keeping me from the summit and the high mountain campsite that I hoped to reach before dark. Expecting bad weather, I've decided to stay at a trail shelter near the north base of the mountain. However, 14 hikers have already taken over the shelter and the few tent sites; more hikers are expected before nightfall. Unworried, I easily find suitable trees for my hammock on the steep, rocky slope near the shelter. The next day, my hiking companions, who were forced to squeeze into the crowded shelter, complain about the snoring that kept them awake.

Isabella Lake, Quetico Provincial Park, Ontario, Canada
Jun 7, 2000

Had to change my plans today when I paddled across the international border. The folks at the Prairie Portage Canadian Customs station misplaced my backcountry reservation and I am forced to follow a more-crowded route for the next few days. I'm advised that available campsites will be hard to find because of the summer crowds. Thank goodness I have my hammock with me! I passed numerous occupied campsites all day and finally found this secluded spot, which is a beautiful rocky bank high above the lake. No one has ever camped here before since the ground is rocky and steep. My hammock is strung between two trees on the edge of the drop-off; if I get out on the wrong side, I'll fall 60' into the water! Mosquitoes, black flies, and no-see-ums drive me inside. Sunset is spectacular. Three canoes loaded with people call out to inquire if there is room at my site for their tents. I have to tell them no--guess what they will bring next time!

continued

Avoiding Crowded Campsites (Cont'd.)

Highland Beach, Everglades National Park, FL
Feb 10, 1991

Where did all these people come from? I've seen only a few other paddlers the past 6 days along the 99-mile Wilderness Waterway. But as soon as I leave the interior estuaries of the 'Glades and come to the Gulf side beaches, I find hoards of campers; most are motor boaters. Tents stretch the full length of the beach, all exposed to the blazing sun. Luckily, I find a grove of palm trees at the back of the beach. The trees not only offer shade, but also seclusion since the tent users favor the soft sand of the beach to the prickly grass on the ground under the trees. Perfect for my hammock. The sun setting into the Gulf waters is my reward. Raccoons emerge at dusk to roam the beach and raid the tent users; two actually came out of a tree that I am tied to! Bright stars and the lapping surf lull me to sleep.

I never build a campfire, especially at my stealth sites. I may use a small camp stove to cook dinner, but generally I do this even before beginning my search for a campsite. By eating dinner before making camp, I can camp far away from water sources and avoid any potentially troublesome food odors in camp, as well as protect my pristine campsite.

Avoid Tree Damage

The tender bark on young trees can be damaged by hammock ropes, which often stretch and "roll" as they tighten against the tree. This can cause unsightly and potentially harmful bruises on some trees. The one-inch wide low-stretch polypropylene straps used on my hammocks, and the unique four-wrap knot described in an earlier chapter, eliminate this problem. Sturdy live trees four to twelve inches in diameter are ideal for hammock supports. Smaller trees will probably bend too much, while larger trees can be too big around to use the four-wrap knot with the twelve-foot straps supplied with the hammock.

Interaction with Others

The wilderness environment also includes other people. With your newfound freedom as a hammock camper comes the responsibility to avoid disharmony with your fellow travelers. Courtesy and wisdom are always preferable to poor behavior in the wilderness, even more so than they are in town.

For instance, simply because a hammock camper can safely set up on the top of a mountain, does not justify him/her being there the next morning when the first early hikers arrive. Likewise, camping in the middle of a scenic overlook and blocking everyone else's view will never be considered acceptable.

Use your hammock to find secluded sites far from the beaten path where you will not encounter others. Use your imagination to find scenic sites unknown and unused by others. In most forested areas, your imagination is your only limitation.

I have conveniently camped in the forest near the edge of towns so I could easily walk into town early the next morning. Out of the way and out of sight, no one knew I was there, although I was nearby. At other times, I have camped deep in the forest at spots visited only by birds and animals. At these sites far from the beaten path, it's amazing how casual and undisturbed animals are by my presence.

Always abide by any posted camping restrictions, even though they are obviously directed toward tent campers. Many government and private lands have such restrictions, which vary from area to area. Areas posted with "No Trespassing" or "No Camping" signs are also off limits to hammock campers. One of the greatest promises of the Leave No Trace program is the concept that each wilderness user sets an example for others to follow. Be sure your outdoor activities set the right example.

Enjoy the Wilderness with Less Impact

You, too, can start enjoying the wilderness today with less impact. Use a hammock and follow Leave No Trace principles!

Switch to hammock camping and you will be helping the environment

Chapter 5
Hammock Camping Safety

Hammocks can be remarkably safe. This safety however can be compromised. While most people will instinctively understand the dangers involved, this chapter addresses some of them.

What Dangers?

How can a hammock be dangerous? Some dangers of obvious concern include: turning over unexpectedly, catastrophic failure of the hammock materials, hanging knots coming loose, falling trees, falling branches, tripping over the canopy guidelines, walking into the hammock tie-outs, and entanglement in the hammock materials. Undoubtedly other dangers also exist. Thankfully, the user can minimize any potential danger by following some simple procedures. These include such things as being alert to the possibilities of injury, exercising caution, avoiding misuse and abuse of the hammock, and carefully inspecting the entire hammock setup before and during each use.

Hammock Materials

The materials and attachment knots used in my hammocks have been selected for their superior strength and low weight. The balance however, between strength and weight necessarily results in compromises on both sides. While an attempt has been made to ensure safety, absolute safety cannot be guaranteed. Materials may subsequently prove to be unsuitable, deterioration due to use and aging may compromise safety, while the user may knowingly or unknowingly misuse the hammock. To help ensure safety, the hammock user should carefully and frequently inspect all materials for signs of deterioration or incipient failure. Deterioration of the materials that could lead to failure is usually visible long before actual failure occurs; therefore the hammock should be inspected both before and during each use.

Frequent inspection not only helps ensure against catastrophic failure, it also reassures the user that he/she can continue enjoying the comfort and security of the hammock without undue worry.

Keeping the hammock clean can help prevent deterioration of the fabrics by dirt and chemicals such as insect repellant, sunscreen lotions, body oils and sweat. When needed, use any front-loading tumbler-type washing machine. Avoid top-loading agitator-type machines, which greatly tangle all the lines and straps. Most detergents work fine, but you should avoid chlorine bleaches since they cause deterioration of nylon fabrics. The bug net can be safely washed with the hammock. Air drying or using low-temperature settings on machine dryers is recommended. Note that detergent will remove any vapor-proof treatments; therefore, reapply after washing if needed. Generally, there is no need to wash the waterproof rain canopy, but if you do, it may also need retreating.

Like all nylon materials, the hammock and rain canopy will deteriorate with prolonged exposure to UV rays, i.e. the sun. Likewise, the polypropylene hanging straps can be damaged by long-tern exposure to sunlight. Direct sunlight is the most harmful and may compromise safety; but even indirect sunlight can eventually cause problems. Reduce exposure therefore by **never** setting up the hammock or rain canopy in the direct sun and always put them away when not in use. Avoiding as much sunlight and daylight as possible can greatly extend the safe life of the hammock and rain canopy. Discontinue use of any hammock that has been weakened by over-exposure to the sun.

Avoid Misuse

The hammock design presented in this book is intended for one-person use. The extra weight of any additional person will over-stress the setup and could cause serious injury should the hammock or supports fail. Limit the weight in the hammock to its original design; this may include not allowing heavier people to use your hammock. Note that any user who gains weight after acquiring or making a hammock may also be compromising safety!

Do not swing in the hammock. Gentle swaying, described in an earlier chapter, is probably safe; however, anything else may be dangerous.

Avoid sudden heavy movements in the hammock. These can cause extremely strong stresses, far greater than those caused by normal, gentle movements. The greater stresses can cause catastrophic failure of the hammock materials or the sudden release of dead branches overhead as the stresses are transmitted up the support trees and are then amplified even more by the trees' movement. I've actually had the unsuspected dead top of a tree come crashing down simply because I turned over quickly! Avoid quick movements and be sure of your supports.

Punctures to the hammock fabric should be avoided. Even small punctures can greatly weaken the fabric and may lead to catastrophic failure. Punctures during setting up or taking down can result from snagging on sticks, briers, branches, rocks, logs, etc. Punctures during use can result from snagging by wristwatches, belt buckles, shoes, boots, zippers, eyeglasses, head phones, pens, pencils, flashlights, etc.

The hammock materials are **not** fire retardant; in fact, they will melt in a flame and can even ignite and burn. Avoid all open flames therefore, and do not smoke in the hammock. Do not set up the hammock anywhere near a campfire since sparks can damage it.

When storing your hammock, follow the usual procedures for protecting nylon fabrics, such as avoiding volatile or corrosive chemicals and UV rays (sunlight).

Children

Children, of course, are greatly attracted to hammocks! While hammocks can be perfectly safe for children, my camping hammocks are fragile and may not be capable of withstanding the extra stresses generated by children at play. Children capable of this understanding may safely use my camping hammocks; otherwise, make or purchase the heavier-duty hammocks for children to use.

Hammocks may not be advisable for young infants, especially those incapable of the muscular ability needed to turn over or get out of a hammock. The US Consumer Product Safety Commission has issued several safety warnings and recalls of net hammocks since 1994 after some small children became entangled in the net material. To view these warnings online, go to:

www.cpsc.gov and search on *"baby-hammocks"* and *"mini-hammocks."* Solid-fabric hammocks offer less hazard of entanglement than net hammocks.

Searching the same CPSC web site for *"rope hammocks"* will locate safety warnings about some commercial rope-net type hammocks that failed and caused falling injuries.

Disabilities

Can people with physical disabilities use my camping hammocks safely? In many cases, the answer may be yes. It, of course, probably depends on the extent and type of disability. While I know some people who use hammocks because of their disability, I have little experience with disabled users. My first hammock however was sold to a lower-back sufferer who, after trying the hammock, decided to sleep in it full-time in the bedroom. A thirteen-year hip-sufferer reports, that unlike his bed, my hammock doesn't cause discomfort.

It is my hope that many disabled people will find sleeping in my hammocks easier than sleeping on the ground or in a bed. The physical ability needed to enter and exit the hammock however, may be beyond the capability of some. Disabled users should first determine the suitability of hammock use for themselves before taking one to the backcountry.

Supports

Sturdy supports are an obvious necessity. Generally, my supports are trees, but I have used rocks, roots, posts, railings, and even car doors. Just make sure the supports are up to the task; trees greater than four inches in diameter should be sufficient. The side-pull stress applied by an occupied hammock is tremendous and can easily bring down a dead, weak, or small tree. I had repeatedly tied off to dead trees before realizing my mistake. I've learned now to be more cautious and carefully inspect each tree; choosing non-dead trees is not always as easy as it sounds. Be very cautious here.

Falling branches also offer potential dangers. High wind, ice and especially the vibrations caused when a hammock is hanging from a tree can release dead branches. Of course, gravity eventually brings down all dead branches anyway, including the very biggest ones. Avoid these dangers by careful inspection before setting up the hammock.

Height Above the Ground

The action of getting into or out of a hammock can be a moment of great instability since the user can easily loose their balance (see below). The unoccupied hammock therefore should not be set up higher than the waist height of the user. The height should be readjusted if shorter people, such as young children, subsequently use the hammock. Trying to get in and out of a hammock above one's waist height requires jumping up or leaping down, which is very dangerous and can lead to personal injury and/or damage to the hammock.

Tipping Over

The tendency of some hammocks to tip over while being occupied has been mentioned in an earlier chapter. The Speer hammocks, based on the design given in this book, are not prone to overturning during normal use such as sitting, lounging or sleeping. In fact, they are amazingly stable without the tipsy feelings inherent to some other hammocks. In any event, with effort the hammocks can be leaned over enough to release the occupant; learn where the tip-over point is and avoid leaning beyond it.

Getting In and Out

The action of getting in or out of the hammock requires extra caution. It's at these times that one is prone to lose balance with the potential of falling and even injury. Once a person has lost balance, there is little chance of recovery since the hammock will generally swing away from the falling person grabbing for support.

Getting in and out of a hammock requires extra caution in much the same way as getting in and out of a canoe does. Backing up to the hammock and gripping it on both sides allows control of the position and level of the hammock as the user maneuvers to get in.

To get in, first sit sideways in the middle of the hammock with your feet still on the ground; this tests the setup before committing your entire weight to the hammock. Generally the hammock fabric, the tie-out straps and the knots give way a bit at this point as they stretch and tighten. I often get up to readjust the straps and inspect the knots and supports at this time. Sit in the hammock again, and when you are convinced the setup will hold, lift your feet, swing them into the hammock and lie back.

Getting out of the hammock is the reverse of getting in; grab both sides of the hammock for leverage and control, then pull yourself up, lift your feet and swing them down to the ground. Stand up only once you're sure your feet are on the ground, your legs will take your full weight and your balance is secure.

Tripping and Entanglements

Walking around a hammock can lead to running into the hanging straps or tripping over the guidelines if the rain canopy is deployed. Brightly colored guidelines are recommended since they are especially helpful in the low-light conditions when tripping is most likely. Using or exercising extra caution when walking near the hammock can help prevent these types of accidents.

Entanglements in the hammock materials can also cause injury. The danger is probably greatest when the hammock and/or rain canopy are lying on the ground during set up and take down. The slippery fabrics and numerous long straps and guidelines can easily entangle feet and hands and lead to injury. Being extra cautious at these times can prevent these problems.

While entanglement inside the hammock is unlikely, it is possible. Bulky clothes, sleeping bags and sleep pads can add to the problem. The bug net or bug net support line could become entangled in clothes or hair or other items inside the hammock. The hook and loop attachment strips on the bug net, hammock, or sleeping bag could entangle fabrics, lines, etc. Using extra caution can help keep these minor nuisances from becoming dangerous.

Carry a Whistle

OK, you've used your imagination and set up your hammock at an unseen location off the beaten path, but something unexpected has happened and you now need to attract the attention of others for help. A small loud whistle may save the day. Carry it attached to your pack or hammock for handy access.

Enjoy Your Hammock Safely

You can enjoy your hammock safely and comfortably by exercising simple caution and common sense. No "technical" or special training is necessary. Although the hammock itself is remarkably simple, no additional gear is needed. The set up procedures are easier than setting up a tent and they are quickly learned; everyone is up and running (or should I say "sleeping"?) the first time!

Chapter 6
How To Make
Your Own Hammock

Consider first how slight a shelter is absolutely necessary

Henry David Thoreau **Walden**

The really good news is that making your own hammock is simple and inexpensive. An extremely suitable wilderness-use hammock shelter can be made with a sewing machine, about $100 in mail-order materials, and a few days of effort.

In this chapter you will learn everything you need to make your own hammock. Imagine the joy of sleeping in your own creation, while being warmer, drier, and more comfortable than anyone else in the wilderness! Making and using your own gear is extremely satisfying and can change your usual outdoor ordeals into the pleasant experiences you hoped for.

Anyone Can Sew It!
No previous sewing experience is required to make one of my hammocks and most people will have no problem with the little sewing that is required. The sewing is

essentially limited to easy edge hems and a few straight seams.

Some people however, might need assistance. Adequate instructional manuals are readily available at all sewing centers or fabric suppliers. In addition, some informative Internet sites are listed below.

General Sewing and Fabric Web Sites

Fabrics.net
www.fabrics.net

Sewing and Repair for Outdoor Enthusiasts
www.specialtyoutdoors.com

Fashion Sewing Internet Connections
www.pages.prodigy.net/shereemckee/fashion.htm

The Fabric Directory
www.interiormall.com

Sewing Machine
Any working household sewing machine will do nicely. Heavy-duty industrial models are not necessary.

Needles
The same needle you use for normal sewing is probably suitable for the lighter hammock fabrics. The heavier fabrics used in the sturdier hammocks however, may require stronger needles; some suggested needles are given later in this chapter. Don't worry however, about having the perfect needle. If the needle breaks, it's the wrong one; try a stronger one. Check your sewing basket, since many people already have a variety of needles to choose from. If necessary, consult the manual

for your machine and buy a stronger one, or a variety pack, at the nearest sewing center or fabric store and resume sewing. Needles can also be mail-ordered from the suppliers listed in this chapter.

Sewing Machine

Although thick, the polypropylene straps do not require extra strong needles when being sewed since they are not dense; just be careful when making reinforced stitches since the density does increase with each new stitch and you can easily exceed the needle-breaking point.

Sharp needles work best, so you may want to start with a new one.

Thread

Use 100% polyester thread in regular strength, as it is sun, mildew and abrasion resistant. It is also strong and non-water-absorbent. Güterman brand is one wise choice since it is approximately the same diameter as normal thread. It should work in most machines without the need to change needles or adjust the tension (a task best avoided if possible). The fabric suppliers listed in this chapter sell many suitable brands, including Güterman. Less-expensive discount brands are also available; just make sure to purchase 100% polyester.

Avoid the more common cotton-covered polyester or mixed cotton-polyester threads found in all fabric stores since they will absorb water, which greatly delays drying time in the field. They also quickly rot in outdoor conditions.

Choose thread colors to match or accent the hammock fabrics. Black is always acceptable.

Stitch Length

All machines provide for adjusting the stitch length; if needed, consult your manual. For hemming edges, set the length to normal sewing (10 to 15 stitches per inch or 2.5mm to 3.5mm long stitches). For doing seams or attaching Velcro, set the length for reinforced sewing (18 to 20 stitches per inch or 2.0mm to 2.5mm long stitches).

Materials List

All the materials needed for your hammock are listed in the table that follows. The costs are approximates based on 2002 prices.

It is a good idea to calculate the full amount of materials needed and be sure to order the proper amount. There is nothing worse than getting into the project just to realize you need to pause because you don't have enough of some critical item, such as Velcro or thread.

Chapter 6 Make Hammock - 111

Materials List and Typical Costs

- **Hammock**
  - Fabric: breathable nylon, 5-6 yd^2 — $12-30
  - Straps: 1 or 1.5 in polypropylene webbing, 24 ft — $ 3
  - Attachment strips: 3/4 in Velcro loop, 18 ft — $ 5
  - D rings: 1 in, 2 — $ 0.25
- **Bug Net**
  - Fabric: no-see-um netting, 100% polyester, 1.0 oz/ yd^2 , 2-3 yd^2 — $ 9
  - Attachment strips: 3/4 in Velcro hook, 18 ft — $ 5
  - Support line: 1/16 in Spectra Pulse Line, 18 ft — $ 3
- **Rain Canopy**
  - Fabric: 1.1 oz/yd^2 silicone coated nylon, 9 yd^2 — $30
  - Pull-tabs: 1 in Grosgrain Nylon Ribbon, 1/2 yd — $ 1
  - Guidelines: 1/16 in Spectra Pulse Line, 60 ft — $ 9
- **Thread**
  - 100% Polyester, color/s of choice — $ 2

See the discussions below to determine the length of the hammock and the load-carrying capacity suited to you. This will determine the actual amount of fabrics, bug net support line, and Velcro attachment strips needed for your hammock. In addition, your fabric strength selection will determine which hammock bottom fabric to use.

Choosing Hammock Fabric

Strength is the primary consideration when choosing fabric for the hammock bottom. Of course, texture and airflow are also important; some people would also include color.

The lighter fabrics mentioned below (i.e. the 70-denier nylons) are easily punctured when stretched tight in an occupied hammock. While use by a careful adult camper will generally not damage these fabrics, the tougher 2.5 to 4.5 oz/yd^2 Supplex or Cordura fabrics might be more appropriate for children who may be less careful.

Polyurethane- or silicone-coated non-breathable fabrics are generally unsuited for multiple-season hammock use. Several of the fabrics suggested below however, come with DWR (Durable Water Resistant) coating, which is acceptable since the coating can be easily removed by washing when not needed and then reapplied when it is needed.

Fabric Strength

While there are no industry strength standards that we can use to make decisions, a rough estimate of fabric strength can generally be judged by the fabric's **material, denier, thread count,** and **weight per square yard**. These features are usually, but not always, given in the fabric's catalog description.

Nylon **material** is used in all of my hammocks. It is especially well-suited for outdoor use and is lightweight, strong, resistant to abrasion, has low stretch, and is quick-drying.

Denier refers to the diameter and weight, but not necessarily the strength, of the individual thread in the fabric. Higher-denier numbers however, generally relate to stronger thread and, therefore, stronger fabrics.

Thread count refers to the actual number of threads per unit of length. A higher tread count means a greater number of threads and a tighter weave. This generally means greater fabric strength.

Fabric Weight

The **weight per square yard** can be most useful, generally indicating greater strength as the weight per square yard increases. Be aware that weight per square yard, as well as texture, can vary greatly between different colors of the same fabric. Read the catalog descriptions carefully and/or call the supplier if final weight is critical to you.

Fabrics are often described by their weight per square yard, such as 1.9 oz/yd². Note however, that this measurement is generally shorted in conversations or catalog descriptions in the US as "weight per yard", without the square notation. Fabric weights in countries other than the US can refer to vastly different measurements (buyer beware).

When calculating weights, note that a yard of fabric, as it is purchased from a US supplier, is not a square yard. Fabric is manufactured and sold in various widths; therefore, it is priced by the running yard, not by the square yard. As noted above however, fabric weight is given by the square yard, although the word square is often omitted.

Since fabric catalog descriptions can be confusing, the guidelines in the following table might be useful. They are based on the weight of the hammock user while trying to achieve low overall hammock weight.

These aren't the only fabrics suitable for hammocks; undoubtedly there are many more. These are only suggestions based on my experience. Of course, every hammock maker should exercise caution when following these suggestions; reject any fabric that you do not feel comfortable with. When purchasing ripstop nylon, **do not** confuse the 1.9 oz/yd² fabric recommended for hammocks with its lighter 1.1 oz/yd² cousin, which is recommended only for the rain canopy (see below).

Choosing Hammock Bottom Fabric

- **If you weigh less than 200 pounds**
  1) 70-denier, 1.9 oz/yd^2 breathable ripstop nylon; or
  2) 70-denier (or 160X90 tread count) breathable nylon
       Taffeta in 2.2-2.5 oz/yd^2 weights
  Allow 24 inches for tying the end knots
  Suggested needle: Universal 70/10

- **If you weight between 200 and 300 pounds**
  Breathable Supplex nylon in 2.5 to 3.5 oz/yd^2 weights
  Allow 28 inches for tying the end knots
  Suggested needle: Universal 80/12

- **If you weigh between 300 and 350 pounds**
  Breathable Cordura nylon in 3.5 to 4.5 oz/yd^2 weights
  Allow 30 inches for tying the end knots
  Suggested needle: Universal 80/12

Calculating Fabric Weight

Often fabric weight is not specified by the seller, especially fabric sold off-the-shelf in retail stores. The buyer is left wondering if the material is strong enough for hammocks. You can calculate the fabric weight yourself, although it requires purchasing a sizable piece of material and taking it home to weigh on an accurate scale. A digital postage scale that measures to the nearest tenth of an ounce works fine and can be purchased from an office supply retailer. First, weigh a rectangular piece of fabric, just as it comes from the store; the larger it is, the more accurate the calculation will be. Then determine the total area (in square inches) of the piece by measuring its long and short sides (in inches). Then, using the formulas in the information box that follows, calculate the weight per square yard (wt/yd^2).

Calculating Fabric Weight

Here is a formula for calculating the weight of a square yard of fabric. Since we know that $1yd^2 = 1,296\ in^2$, we can take any large piece of fabric with known length, width and weight and figure out the weight per square yard

$$\underline{\hspace{3cm}} \quad X \quad \underline{\hspace{3cm}} \quad = \quad \underline{\hspace{3cm}}$$
length (in) $\qquad$ width (in) $\qquad$ area (in^2)

$$\underline{\hspace{3cm}} \quad = \quad \underline{\hspace{3cm}}$$
area (in^2) $\qquad$ weight (oz)

$$\underline{\hspace{3cm}} \quad \text{divided by } 1,296\ in^2 = \underline{\hspace{3cm}}$$
area (in^2) $\qquad$ area (yd^2)

$$\underline{\hspace{3cm}} \quad \text{divided by } \underline{\hspace{3cm}} \quad = \quad \underline{\hspace{3cm}}$$
weight (oz) $\qquad$ area (yd^2) $\qquad$ weight/yd^2

$$1yd^2 = \underline{\hspace{3cm}} \text{ weight/}yd^2$$

Example
   If the length of the fabric is 144 inches (in)
   If the width of the fabric is 60 inches (in)
   If the weight of the fabric is 22.6 ounces (oz)

$$144\ in\ X\ 60\ in = 8,640\ in^2$$
$$8,640\ in^2 = 22.6\ oz$$
$$8,640\ in^2 \text{ divided by } 1,296\ in^2 = 6.67\ yd^2$$
$$22.6\ oz \text{ divided by } 6.67\ yd^2 = 3.4\ oz/yd^2$$
$$1yd^2 = 3.4\ oz.yd^2$$

This fabric weighs $3.4\ oz/yd^2$

If you don't have access to an accurate scale, you probably can make a reasonable guess of the fabric weight by comparing it to catalog descriptions of similar fabric. Alternately, most of the mail order suppliers listed below sell sample swatches of their fabrics; these can be useful when considering an unknown fabric.

Fabric Color

Choosing the color of your hammock is important. Most campers find dark colors depressing, especially after several days of cold dreary rain and fog in the outback. Use light natural colors for easier moods. Have you ever noticed that most tents are made out of various muted shades of blue, tan, gray, green or yellow? The reason is that these colors are less depressing than dark or bright shades of green, red, orange, purple, or other exotic colors. While a wide variety of colors is available to choose from, light natural colors will probably be more pleasing in the long run.

For those interested, camouflage nylon fabrics are available from many fabric suppliers.

Remember, you will also be choosing the color of the thread, the hanging straps and the rain canopy. Choose colors that accent or compliment each other. For a more professional look, colored accent trim can be added to the hammock and rain canopy edges.

The choice of the rain canopy color is even more important than that of the hammock. See the Rain Canopy section later in this chapter.

Fabric Sources

Nylon fabrics suitable for hammocks can be purchased from local or mail-order suppliers (see list below). Although mail-order suppliers often have greater selections, local suppliers may have better prices. Note

Mail-Order Sources for
Hammock Fabrics

Nylon Fabrics, No-See-Um Netting and Webbing
Fabric weights, textures, colors and prices vary greatly;
compare before buying

American Home & Habitat
10400 Courthouse Road PMB 274
Spotsylvania, VA 22553
540-710-9249
www.americanhomeandhabitat.com
Email: info@americanhomeandhabitat.com

Emerald Citi Textile, Inc.
3322 16th St.
Everett, WA 98201
888-343-1220
www.ectextile.com
Email: info@ectextile.com

Outdoor Threads
1808 Belmont Ave.
Hood River, OR 97031
541-386-5445
www.outdoorthreads.com
Email: sales@outdoorthreads.com

Outdoor Wilderness Fabrics, Inc.
16415 Midland Blvd.
Nampa, ID 83687
800-693-7467
www.owfinc.com
Email: owfinc@owfinc.com

Quest Outfitters
4919 Hubner
Sarasota, FL 34241
800-359-6931
www.questoutfitters.com
Email: questoutfitters@home.com

continued

Mail-Order Sources for Hammock Fabrics (Cont'd.)

Seattle Fabrics, Inc.
8702 Aurora Ave. N
Seattle, WA 98103
206-525-0670
www.seattlefabrics.com

Textile Outfitters
735 10th Ave. SW
Calgary, AB
Canada T2R 0B3
403-543-7677
www.justmakeit.com
Email: moreinfo@justmakeit.com

The Rain Shed, Inc.
707 NW 11th
Corvallis, OR 97330
541-753-8900

that the no-see-um bug netting, polypropylene webbing, and Velcro are generally available only through mail order.

Discount Fabrics

Discounted nylon fabrics, often sold at huge price savings, may be found at local fabric retailers, discount outlets, and variety retailers like Wal-Mart, as well as the specialty mail-order houses listed below. Although selections may be limited, checking the local sources first can lead to prices considerably less than those given above. I've found suitable hammock fabrics for as little as $1 per yard at discount tables.

Caution: These discounted fabrics are generally second quality, which may or may not compromise fabric strength. Often the blemishes are only unnoticeable color or texture variations, but defective or weakened material may also occur. These discounted second-quality fabrics lend themselves to inexpensive experimenting since you can make several hammocks from different materials, or hammocks of different sizes. When in doubt however, always opt for stronger material.

You may want to make a simple inexpensive hammock from discounted fabric (often only $5-$12 total); this is a good way to try hammocks at home before committing to the more-expensive fabrics suggested above. Like some people, you may find no reason to switch to the higher-cost fabrics.

Hammock Size

The interior of your finished hammock should be two feet longer than your height. Thus, your unfinished hammock fabric length should be two feet longer than your height plus the allowance for tying the end knots (see the sections "Hammock End Knots" and "Tying Hammock End Knots" later in this chapter). Also factor in any allowance your want for hems (1.5" on each edge is recommended). Use the worksheet below to determine the actual cut length of your hammock. Now cut the fabric at the proper length; an inch or two either way is not critical.

All of my hammock designs are five feet wide, which is generally the width of the fabric as it comes from the supplier. That's right, you probably won't have to cut the fabric for the width! If your fabric is an inch or two wider or narrower, you can use it as is. If your fabric width is greater by more than a few inches, you may want to cut it to the suggested five-foot width.

Don't however use fabric that is not wide enough by itself. In other words, don't splice fabric panels together to get the suggested width. Doing so will create a very uncomfortable "reinforced ridgeline" in the hammock bottom. In addition, sewed seams in the lighter-weight fabrics are dangerous and are prone to failure (the fabric fails along the needle holes at the seam, not the stitching itself). For comfort and safety, the entire hammock bottom should be a single piece of fabric.

Calculating Your Hammock Length

Here is a worksheet for calculating the cut length of your hammock bottom fabric

Your height
plus 2 ft
plus allowance for tying end knots
plus allowance for hems

Below 200 lbs

_____ + 2 ft + 24 in + 3 in = _____
your height   length of cut fabric

200-300 lbs

_____ + 2 ft + 28 in + 3 in = _____
your height   length of cut fabric

300-350 lbs

_____ + 2 ft + 30 in + 3 in = _____
your height   length of cut fabric

Example
My height is 5 ft 11 in; my weight is 170 lbs
Thus: 5 ft 11 in + 2 ft + 24 in + 3 in = 10 ft 2 in
My hammock bottom fabric should be cut 10 ft 2 in long

Note: anything within a few inches of this number will work fine

If your fabric has different textures on each side, decide which texture you want on the inside and which you want on the outside of your hammock (it generally doesn't make any difference, but I choose to put the less-slick side inside if possible).

Any unraveling edges should now be secured before proceeding further. While some fabrics come with secured edges already, many do not, and all scissor cuts in nylon material will quickly unravel. You can secure the edges by hemming them 1 to 1 1/2 inches. If you are lucky enough to have a serger machine, you can easily serge the edges (be sure to use 100% polyester thread).

Attach Velcro to Hammock Edges

The bug net is attached to the hammock by Velcro strips. It is best if the strips on the hammock are sewed on next.

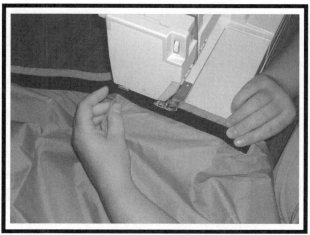

Attaching Velcro to Hammock

122 - Hammock Camping

The soft Velcro loop strips will be sewed to the edges of the hammock fabric. Cut two strips; each should be your height plus two feet in length (note this is considerably shorter than the length of your hammock fabric). Pin the strips along the outside edges of the hammock fabric. Position the Velcro strips so they do not extend into the end allowances for tying the end knots; in other words, the Velcro strips should stop 12 to 15 inches from the end of the hammock fabric (depends on the length of material allowed for tying the end knots). Sew the strips to the hammock; two stitched seams, one on each side of the Velcro strip, should be sufficient.

Velcro attachment strips can be ordered from the same suppliers as the hammock fabric. Remember to order both the hook and loop strips. Less expensive generic brands are available from some retailers.

Hammock End Knots

The hammock fabric is attached to the hanging straps by tying simple overhand knots at each end of the hammock. While the hammock knots certainly don't look regal, they are surprisingly strong. In fact, they are much stronger than sewing fabric loops at the ends of the hammock for attaching the hanging straps. Sewed loops have failed me on all but the heaviest hammock fabrics! In fact, you should avoid sewed seams anywhere inside your hammock.

Failure along sewed seams often is not immediate, but slowly develops over weeks or months of use. The tight-weave nylon fabrics used in my hammocks are strong enough to support the user's weight, but the lighter ones will often pull apart along sewed seams after extended use; therefore, I avoid sewed seams in all my hammocks. Some commercial hammocks suffer from this delayed phenomenon (buyer beware!).

My overhand end knots however, are safer since they are strong without putting undue stress on the fabric. The knots actually allow the use of lighter weight fabrics that otherwise would fail along sewed seams.

Each hanging strap is looped around the hammock side of a hammock end knot and is securely stitched together as explained in the section "Polypropylene Straps".

Tying Hammock End Knots

The overhand end knots are tied in the hammock fabric just as similar knots would be tied in ropes. The picture sequence should be helpful. To begin, fold the hammock fabric in half lengthwise, similar to how it will look when in use.

Hold one end of this folded fabric in each hand as shown in the accompanying pictures; your right hand should hold the fold edge and your left hand should hold the two hammock edges together (hopefully you are right-handed like I am!). Using your fingers, now gather the fabric in folds in your right hand; keep the ends of the gathered folds even with each other. When your right hand is about five inches from your left hand, continue gathering this last five inches into your right hand but pull these folds two inches beyond the end of the other folds (this causes the sides of the finished hammock to stand up; it makes sides on the hammock and helps prevent the user from falling out). Now follow the picture sequence and complete the overhand knot. Work the knot to within one-half inch of the end of the fabric before final tightening. Make the knot as compact and snug as possible; don't worry, it will not come loose or slip during use.

The end knot can usually be untied and retied several times as necessary for final adjustments, but once the hammock is occupied a few times the knot will probably tighten too much to undo.

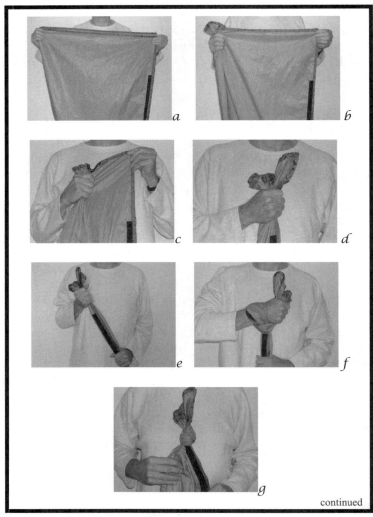

continued

Tying Hammock End Knots

a. Fold hammock lengthwise, notice Velcro strip on long edge. Dark accent trim used here on fabric edges to enhance photographs
b. Gather folds in right hand
c. Last 5 inches, notice the accent trim on fabric edges
d. Pull last folds 2 inches longer than previous folds
e. Begin overhand knot, notice Velcro strip
f. Tie overhand knot
g. Finished knot, notice Velcro strip passing into knot

Tying Hammock End Knots (Cont'd.)

Following the same procedure, tie the knot on the other end of the hammock. Next, attach the hanging straps as described below.

Polypropylene Straps

Polypropylene webbing straps are used for the hammock tie-outs because of their low-memory stretch and flat width that do not harm tree bark. Avoid nylon webbing since its' high-memory stretch makes it impossible to set up the hammock with the proper tension. Polypropylene straps can be purchased from the same fabric suppliers listed in the information box.

Beware of inferior webbing. The strength of any webbing depends on its thickness, weave and size of fibers as well as its' width; thus, not all 1"-wide webbing is equally strong. Polypropylene webbing is generally listed with tensile strengths as low as 200 or as high as 700 lbs/in. This means 1"-wide webbing from different manufactures or suppliers may vary in breaking strength as much as 500 pounds! Call the supplier and only accept webbing with strengths greater than 600 pounds.

Since the strength is given as pounds per inch, the breaking strength of webbing wider or narrower than 1" must be calculated; i.e., a 1/2" strap has only 50% of the strength while a 1.5" strap has 150% of the listed tensile strength. I've broken 1/2" straps before, but have never broken the 700 pound 1" straps.

Remember that the weight of the occupied hammock is held by two straps; thus, the weight on any one strap is half the user's weight. The dynamic stresses however, caused by movements inside the hammock, can greatly exceed the user's weight. Users heavier than 250 pounds will probably want to use the stronger 1.5"-wide straps.

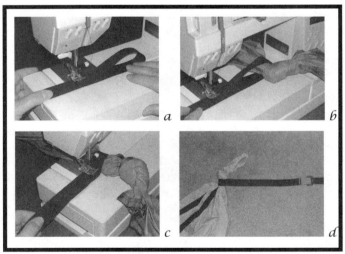

Attaching Polypropylene Straps

Attach the polypropylene straps as shown in the picture sequence above. Sewed straps are stronger than tying knots in the straps (a lesson learned from rock climbers). The straps are attached by sewing loops (picture a) around the hammock just inside the hammock end knots (picture b). It is important here to stitch the loop in each hanging strap as close to the hammock as possible in order to prevent the loop from slipping over the hammock end knot when it is loaded and stretched (pictures c & d). When occupied, each hanging strap will pull at an angle to the hammock end knot, thus ensuring security.

Seeping Rainwater

Heavy rains can cause water to run or soak down the hanging straps and into the hammock. Although rare, this is a serious problem when it does happen. This is most likely during the winter months when trees have dropped their leaves and rainwater is now funneled down the limbs and trunks of the trees rather than being dispersed to drip off by the leaves. Polypropylene webbing is hydrophobic and does not absorb water (it even floats!). Water however, can run down the surface of the webbing and can also slowly seep along and between the fibers, finally reaching the hammock.

Liner Sock Used to Stop Seeping Rainwater

Two bandanas or a pair of socks can block this unwanted water. Tie them around each strap between the hammock and the tree, making sure that both sides of the strap are in contact with the sock or bandana (i.e. don't allow the strap to fold back to itself). Thin nylon liner socks, generally carried in the pack anyway and probably in need of a good washing, work great. Yes, they may get wet, but they are easier to deal with than having water in the hammock. They quickly dry once the rain has stopped. Instead of packing them away wet, hang them on a rock, a bush or the outside of your pack.

Now you are ready to test your hammock.

Test Hammock

Set up your hammock following the directions in Chapter 1, "The Joy and Comfort of Hammock Camping" and Appendix 2, Tips for Hammock Camping. Always be extra cautious when testing a new hammock or setup. Double-check the supports, the hammock end knots, the hanging straps, and the tree knots. Add your weight slowly to the hammock; readjust the hanging straps if necessary before committing your full weight.

This is the time to make sure the sidewalls of the hammock are sufficient without being too tight; if too tight, the hammock sides stand up too much and make sitting sideways in the hammock uncomfortable. If sitting sideways is comfortable, the sidewalls are not too tight. Excessively high sidewalls will also hinder the use of a sleeping bag rigged around the hammock. If necessary, retie the end knots with less tension on the long edges of the hammock--do this now because after too much pressure is applied by occupying the hammock, you will not be able to untie the knots.

Is the hammock long enough? If not, can the knots be retied closer to the ends of the fabric, thus giving more interior space? Remember, this may be the last time you will be able to adjust the end knots.

Try pitching the hammock with different amounts of sag; you will quickly learn which position is best. Try supports with different widths.

If everything meets your approval, take a nap! You've earned it! Next, we will make the bug net.

Bug Net

The bug net is made from 100% polyester no-see-um netting, which again can be ordered from the same suppliers as the hammock fabric. Regular mosquito netting should be avoided since it has openings large enough to allow the smaller biting gnats and flies to enter. Black netting reflects and scatters less incoming light than lighter colored netting, thus it is easier to see through from up close, and should be the netting of choice.

The bug net fabric weighs about 1.0 oz/yd^2 and can easily be sewed with a Universal 70/10 or equivalent needle.

The ends of the finished bug net must extend beyond the ends of the hammock. Cut the length of the bug net therefore, so it extends about three inches beyond each end of the finished hammock. The actual length, of course, depends on the length of your finished hammock. Simply lay the fully stretched hammock on the floor and cut the bug net length accordingly.

The finished width of the bug net should be about 24 inches, but anything within two inches of this will work fine.

Secure the edges of the no-see-um netting with 1"-wide hems; these wide hems will reinforce the fabric where the Velcro is attached.

The bug net is attached to the hammock by 3/4"-wide Velcro strips. There are two sides of the Velcro strips, one with stiff hooks and the other with soft loops. Since the stiff hook strip easily catches on clothing, it is sewed to the bug net, which helps keep it out of the way of the user's clothes as he/she gets in and out of the hammock.

Sew the Velcro coarse hook strips to the two inside edges of the bug net; two stitched seams, one on each side of the Velcro strip, should be sufficient.

Next, Velcro strips should also be sewed to the ends of the bug net as shown in the picture. This allows the ends of the bug net to be easily opened or closed as needed to secure the ends of the bug net around the hammock hanging straps (see picture).

Once the bug net support line is installed (see below), your bug net is finished!

Bug Net Support Line

The bug net support line holds the bug net above the hammock and provides interior space. It is made from one-sixteenth-inch Spectra Pulse Line, which is a stiff, solid core, nylon sheath cord with great strength (275 pound) and low-tangle qualities. It is bright pink, which makes it easy to see in low-light conditions. Since each hammock setup is different, the bug net support line is adjustable, which allows the user to maximize the space inside the hammock by raising or lowering the bug net as needed. The support line can also be loosened and moved out of the way when the hammock is used as a chair or a sleeping bag is positioned around the hammock.

The recommended bug net support line material can be ordered from the marine suppliers listed below.

Sources for Support Line and Guidelines

Spectra Pulse Line, pink 1/16" by Yale Cordage, Inc.

Boat US
800-937-2628
www.boatus.com
Email: catalogsales@boatus.com
Item # 102218

West Marine
PO Box 50070
Watsonville, CA 95077-0070
800-BOATING
www.westmarine.com
Email: webmaster@westmarine.com
Model # 543861

At first, the bug net support line should be 17-18 feet long; you may later trim it to suit yourself, but be careful since different hammock setups require different support line lengths.

The ends of the bug net support line are attached to the hammock hanging straps (see pictures below). Each attachment point should be 12 inches beyond the end of the hammock.

Make the attachment anchors by sewing 2" lengths of webbing (cut from the ends of each hanging strap) to the hanging straps; inserting 1" D rings as shown in the pictures. Each 2" length of webbing should be sewed securely to the hanging strap with multiple reinforced stitches. The plastic D rings can be ordered from the same fabric suppliers listed earlier.

One end of the bug net support line is simply tied to one D ring. The other end of the support line is passed through the other D ring and looped back inside the hammock. The pictures should help.

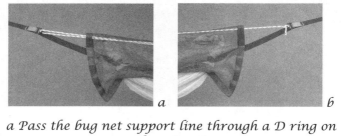

a Pass the bug net support line through a D ring on one hanging strap
b Tie the other end of bug net support line to the other D ring

Attaching Bug Net Support Line to Hammock Straps

Next tie a trucker's hitch in the middle of the bug net support line by tying a two-inch overhand-knot loop and pass the loose end of the support line through this loop. Pull the loose end tightly against the loop and tie it off (see the picture below and those under the **Trucker's Hitch** section later in this chapter).

Once you get into your hammock, you can easily adjust the bug net support line to the preferred tension, which is just enough to hold the bug net above the hammock. Note that the bug net support line is not designed to alter the sag or to support any of the weight of the occupied hammock; allowing it to do so can damage the support line, the D rings or the bug net.

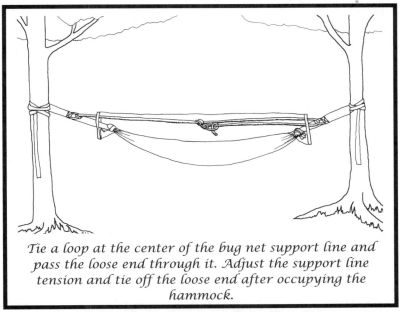

Tie a loop at the center of the bug net support line and pass the loose end through it. Adjust the support line tension and tie off the loose end after occupying the hammock.

Tying Trucker's Hitch in Bug Net Support Line

Note that the bug net support line should be loosened before the hammock is set up each time, since often the previously set support line can now be under great tension with the new setup. The support line should only be tightened after the hammock is occupied, which is easily done from inside. Adjust the support line so that it holds the bug net above the hammock; secure it with an easy-to-undo slipknot. The loose end of the line can now be tucked out the way by looping it over the support line. The bug net now hangs well above the hammock and provides ample interior space. Small items such as bandanas, flashlights or eyeglasses can be conveniently suspended from the line.

.To complete installing the bug net support line, it is now passed through the Velcro ends of the bug net so that it holds the bug net above the occupied hammock (see pictures).

Last, we will make the rain canopy.

Rain Canopy

The eight-by-ten foot rain canopy is made from 40-denier, 1.1 oz/yd^2 silicone-coated ripstop nylon, which is extremely strong yet lightweight. Note that this fabric weighs approximately 1.3 oz/yd^2 after the silicone coating has been applied. The material can be ordered from the fabric suppliers listed in the information box. When ordering, be sure you do not confuse this fabric with its heavier 1.9 oz/yd^2 cousin.

As mentioned earlier, choosing the color of the rain canopy is extremely important; this is the most critical color decision you will have to make. With the canopy deployed over you, your camp will be constantly bathed in light that is filtered and tinted by the color of the canopy. Avoid the overly depressing dark or bright shades of non-natural colors; instead choose psychologically-uplifting colors, such as light muted shades of blue, tan, green, gray, or yellow.

The availability of suitable light shades of this fabric is limited and you may need to check several suppliers to find the right color.

You can generally use second-quality silicone-coated fabrics, which cost considerably less than first quality fabrics. Although unlikely, any short fall in the silicone coating can be easily mediated by treating the finished rain canopy with inexpensive spray-on silicone (see the section on "Waterproofing the Rain Canopy" below).

Since this fabric generally comes in five-foot widths, purchase 5 1/3 yards (16 feet) and cut two eight-by-five foot panels, which will be joined together to get the finished eight-by-ten foot size.

By sewing the two panels together, the canopy will have a central transverse seam as shown in the accompanying diagram. While the seam is reinforced and strong, it must still be sealed in order to make it fully waterproof (see instructions below). Note that about one inch on the outside edges of the pre-cut coated fabric generally has tiny perforation holes and lacks full silicone coating; these unsuitable edges should be trimmed off on the edges used to join the two panels to make the center seam. Otherwise, the central seam may not be waterproof.

The perforated and uncoated edges on the outer edges of the finished canopy are also not waterproof, however these edges will be hemmed anyway and will not adversely affect the finished rain canopy. Note that if your fabric is wider than five feet (60 inches), as some are, you could safely trim away all of these perforated and uncoated edges and still have a finished canopy of eight by ten feet.

It's easier to cut each fabric panel exactly eight-by-five foot, rather than trying to calculate seam and hem allowances. In other words, the finished rain canopy may be slightly less than eight-by-ten foot.

Most fabrics have visibly different textures on each side; i.e., they have a top and bottom, or a front and back; as commonly used in sewing terminology, these are the "right" and "wrong" sides. If your fabric has obviously different sides, you will probably want to make sure the two panels being joined together have matching sides, hems and seams. The waterproof-ness of the finished tarp however, will not be compromised in any event, since the silicone treatment has soaked through the thin nylon fabric and is not restricted to the side it was originally applied to.

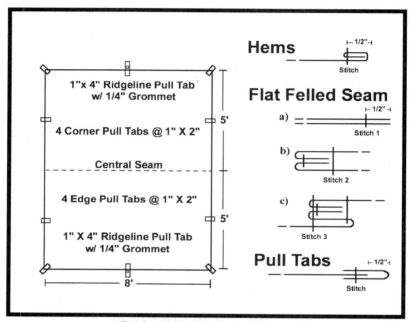

Rain Canopy Details

Join the two panels together along the central seam using the reinforced flat felled seam shown in the diagram. Additional help on suitable seams can be found in most sewing manuals or the sewing web sites listed earlier. With up to five layers of fabric, the reinforced center seam is strong, while it neatly secures the fabric edges from unraveling without the need for hemming or serging.

Now secure the outer edges of the 8X10 canopy by serging or by sewing 1/2" hems as suggested by the diagram and picture.

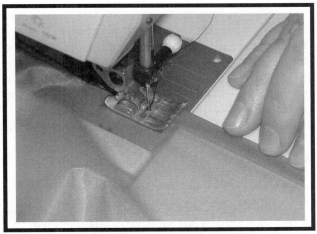

Hemming the Rain Canopy

Pull-Tabs

Pull-tabs for attaching the guidelines are made from one-inch Grosgrain Nylon Ribbon (order from the same fabric suppliers listed in the information box; choose a color that accents your rain canopy material; black always works). You will need four corner pull-tabs, four edge pull-tabs, and two ridgeline pull-tabs. See the earlier diagram for the correct position of the pull-tabs. The eight corner and edge pull-tabs should be two inches long, while the two ridgeline tabs should be four inches long (order 24 inches). Seal the cut ends of each pull-tab by melting them slightly in a small flame.

Attach each pull-tab by folding the ends together and placing it on the rain canopy as shown in the previous diagram; sew the three pieces together. Leave a one-half-inch open loop on the outer end of each pull-tab for attaching the guidelines. Sew at least three reinforcing stitches when attaching the longer ridgeline pull-tabs.

Grommets

You can greatly enhance the use of the rain canopy by setting 1/4" grommets into the ridgeline pull-tabs as shown in the picture. When set up on the ground as a tarp, the grommets accept the tips of your hiking poles (or the ends of sticks) and help keep them in place. See the "Use on the Ground" section in Chapter 2. Grommets and the necessary hand tool can be purchased at many fabric suppliers, including those listed earlier in this chapter.

**Grommet Details and Hiking Pole Used
as Tarp Support on the Ground**

Waterproofing the Rain Canopy

While the silicone-coated rain canopy probably starts out waterproof, actual wilderness use can render it less than watertight. It can however, easily be retreated with spray-on silicone as needed. As mentioned in Chapter 3, inexpensive spray-on silicone treatments can be purchased at most outdoor and sporting goods stores. A single can is sufficient for several coatings. Follow directions on the can and allow the canopy to dry between coatings.

The central seam is not fully waterproof until it is sealed properly by using a silicone-based sealant; many outfitter stores carry this specialty product, but note that regular seam sealant will not adhere properly to this silicone-coated fabric.

An inexpensive sealant can easily be made from a 60/40 mixture of clear household silicone sealant or silicone caulking and a solvent such as gasoline. Any clear silicone sealant or silicone caulking from a hardware or home-improvement store works fine; it can generally be purchased in small squeeze tubes. The solvent can be automobile gasoline or camp stove gasoline; however, extreme caution is necessary when using these highly flammable substances. The solvent dissolves the normally thick silicone sealant or caulking and makes it much easier to spread on the seam, after which the solvent evaporates and leaves the silicone in place. The solvent is not in contact with the nylon fabric long enough to harm it. About 1/4 ounce of this mixture is all it takes to seal both sides of the central seam. Avoid breathing the solvent fumes by working in a well-ventilated area.

Mix the items in a small squeeze bottle using the head of a nail as a plunger/mixer. If necessary, enlarge the spout's exit hole with a straight pin heated in a small flame; hold the hot pin with pliers and keep the flame away from the gasoline! If a suitable squeeze bottle is not available, the items could be mixed on a paper plate and spread over the seam with a plastic picnic knife. Let the sealed seam dry 48 hours and then coat it with baby powder; otherwise it will continually stick to folds of the tarp when stowed away.

Any remaining sealant mixture can be used to protect the stitching on the rain canopy pull-tabs and the polypropylene hanging straps.

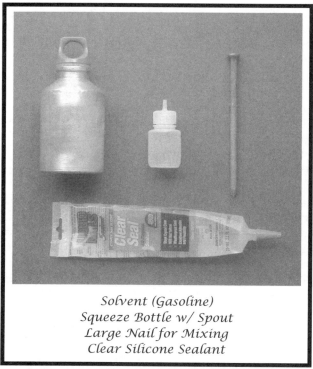

Solvent (Gasoline)
Squeeze Bottle w/ Spout
Large Nail for Mixing
Clear Silicone Sealant

Silicone Seam Sealant Materials

Guidelines

The rain canopy guidelines, like the bug net support line, are made from one-sixteenth inch Spectra Pulse Line. It is bright pink, which makes it easy to see in low-light conditions when tripping over the guidelines is most likely. In addition to the strength, low-tangle, and safety color of the Pulse Line, it is also easy to untie compared to limp cords. This guideline cord can be ordered from the marine suppliers listed earlier in this chapter.

At least six guidelines are required to pitch the rain canopy: four corner guidelines and two ridge guidelines. The cut ends should be secured by slightly melting them in a small flame. Each guideline should be ten feet long for a total of 60 feet of the Pulse Line. The two ridge guidelines are excessively long for pitching the canopy over a hammock, but they are needed when the canopy is pitched like a tarp on the ground. Since all of the Pulse Line guidelines are low-tangle, I save time by leaving them attached to the rain canopy. I simply fold them up with the canopy when breaking camp.

For those times when one cannot hide from strong wind, four extra pull-tabs are attached to the rain canopy, two on each side. To stop the wild flapping caused by strong wind, extra guidelines can be attached to these pull-tabs and secured to the ground or nearby trees. Since these extra guidelines are seldom needed, I use lighter-weight limp line (twisted nylon line available at most hardware or department stores) that I carry separately, even though it tends to tangle easily.

Now attach the six guidelines to the rain canopy. To do this pass one end of the cord through a pull-tab on the canopy making a small loop, which is then tied with an overhand knot (see pictures below). This creates an open loop in the end of the guideline, which passes through the pull-tab.

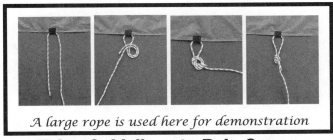

A large rope is used here for demonstration

Tying Guidelines to Rain Canopy

Trucker's Hitch

The trucker's hitch is a handy way to tie off the guidelines to stakes, trees, roots, etc. It allows easy adjustment of the tension on each guideline. See the picture below. It is tied by making a small loop in the standing line using an overhand knot as described above for attaching the guidelines to the rain canopy. Next, the bitter end is passed around the anchor support and then passed back through the loop in the standing line. Now pulling the bitter end backwards toward the anchor support easily sets the tension on the entire guideline. To complete the hitch, a simple quick-release slipknot is tied in the bitter end near the loop in the standing line. The slipknot will be easy to untie even with cold fingers when breaking camp in the morning. The overhand-loop knot in the standing line generally does not tighten excessively and can easily be untied and repositioned as often as necessary.

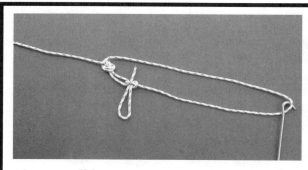

Tie a small loop at an appropriate spot along the guideline and pass the loose end around the anchor. Next pass the loose end through the small loop; adjust the tension and tie off the loose end with an easy-to-untie slipknot. A large rope is used here for demonstration

Tying Trucker's Hitch in Guidelines

Congratulations!

Your hammock is now finished and ready for use. It's time for another nap!

You can be proud of yourself; your creation will give you many years of comfortable outdoor use. You may never sleep on the ground again!

Carry Bags

I generally don't use stuff sacks. Instead, I carry my hammock loose at the bottom of my pack and carry my rain canopy loose in an outside pocket where it is always readily available for quick set up during rainstorms. If you prefer to use carry bags however, they can easily be made. It's a good idea to make them different colors. They should also be a different color than the item inside; this makes them easy to keep track of in the pack or in camp. You can however, also use excess material left over from the original hammock or rain canopy. A finished size of about six-by-nine inches works fine for the rain canopy. The size of the hammock bag however, will vary depending on the weight of the fabric used in your hammock. The ten-by-fifteen inch instructions below can easily be modified as needed for your hammock. Trust your own estimates; they will probably work OK.

For a hammock stuff bag, start by cutting a piece of fabric 20.5 by 16.5 inches. For the best-looking bag, make sure all seams end up on the inside.

Make the drawstring channel next by folding over and sewing a 1.5" hem along the top of the 20.5" edge. Leave at least a 1/2" open channel for the drawstring. Next, join the 16.5" edges by sewing them together, leaving the drawstring channel open; this makes the side seam, and the bag is now a cylinder. Now, sew the bottom edges together and fold the bag inside out so the seams are on the inside. Insert a 13" drawstring, which can be any small cord, by pinning it to a large safety pin and then threading the closed safety pin through the drawstring channel. Finally, anchor the drawstring in place by sewing it to the bag at its mid-point. These bags are so easy to make that you can usually make several of various sizes and colors and use them for clothes, food, etc.

Using an Existing Tarp?

Note that if you intend to use an existing tarp for the rain canopy, it may be necessary to sew on two ridgeline pull-tabs as described above. Having the ridgeline pull-tabs ensures symmetrical set up of the tarp over the hammock; otherwise, it is difficult to get it evenly centered over the hammock.

Setting Up the Rain Canopy

Tie the rain canopy to the same two supports, generally trees that the hammock is attached to. Using a similar four-wrap knot as described in Chapter 1 for attaching the hammock straps will ensure that the canopy ridge guidelines pull from the center of the trees. This helps keep the canopy evenly centered over the hammock and prevents knots that cannot be untied. Follow the picture sequence below.

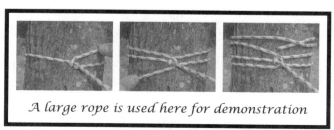

A large rope is used here for demonstration

Tying Canopy Ridge Guidelines to Trees

Next, the corner guidelines can be attached to available trees, bushes, roots, rocks, etc. using the trucker's hitch described earlier. One or both sides of the canopy can be lowered as necessary for added wind or rain protection.

Tips for Reducing Weight Even More!

Although my hammocks are remarkably lightweight, many backpackers, especially long-distance hikers, will be interested in reducing the weight even more. For them, every ounce eliminated means less effort and greater comfort. If you are one of these devoted fanatics (like I am), you probably have already figured out some ways to save weight on my hammocks; however some weight-saving possibilities that may or may not be appropriate for you are given below. The weight of a modified hammock and rain canopy can be as little as 1.2 pounds!

Omitting the bug net and its' support line can save four to six ounces. This is easy since they are removable anyway so that they can be left at home during bug-free seasons. I have used the hammock with only a small piece of bug netting laid over my head during bug season; while not as convenient as the full bug net, it does work and saves some weight. If you intend to never use the bug net, you can save another ounce by omitting the Velcro strips normally sewed to the edges of the hammock.

Trimming the hammock fabric can also save weight with only slight compromise in comfort. The width can be trimmed to four feet instead of the recommended five feet; or the normally rectangular bottom fabric can be cut to an elongated diamond shape (for instance, five feet wide at the mid-point and three and a half feet wide at each end).

The biggest possible weight-savings may come from using lighter than recommended bottom fabrics. **Caution:** This may not work for everyone.

I have successfully tested a lightweight hammock (made from 1.9 oz/yd^2 ripstop with overhand end knots and 1"-wide polypropylene straps) to 170 pounds for months at a time and briefly to 375 pounds. But, since my brief test may not be adequate for extended use, I suggest stronger fabrics and straps for anyone over 250 pounds.

Only you can determine if this approach is safe for you; however the fabrics recommended in this chapter are stronger than they appear and you might want to try several different ones. Of course, you should experiment and thoroughly test such a hammock until you are satisfied with its safety, before heading to the backcountry.

For users less than six feet tall, the hammock can be shortened and the rain canopy can be downsized to seven-by-nine feet with no significant decrease in performance.

Your actual weight savings will, of course, depend on which hammock fabric you choose and which of the above weight-saving possibilities you follow. Weight savings however, up to 30% are possible! Good luck and let me know how your hammock works.

Make your own hammock and be the envy of the wilderness crowd

Chapter 7
How To Buy a
Hammock

This chapter is for those interested in purchasing a camping hammock. Although there are many commercial hammocks available today, remarkably few are suitable for extended wilderness use. In addition, features vary considerably on the ones that are available and this can cause confusion for the first time buyer. In this chapter, reviews of some of the more popular wilderness hammocks give buyers the information they need to make wise decisions.

My intent here is to present all of the suitable wilderness hammocks. There are however, probably some that I am not aware of. If I have missed any maker or manufacturer, please accept my apologies. I will gladly add new information to this review in subsequent editions.

In the **Introduction**, I distinguished between ordinary hammocks and suitable camping hammocks on the basis of six features: 1) comfort, 2) safety, 3) bug protection, 4) storm protection, 5) multiple uses, and 6) weight. The reader of this book should by now understand the differences. It is these six required features that eliminate the vast majority of available hammocks.

Note that it is possible to modify some otherwise unsuitable hammocks for wilderness use; for instance adding a bug net and/or a rain canopy may be all that's required. While these options may be appropriate for some people or some uses, the issues are complex and are not covered here. If you are interested in this option, searching the Internet for *"hammocks"* will generally find many manufactures and suppliers of the more common hammocks. Only complete hammock systems however, are reviewed below.

Although military-type jungle hammocks have been left out of these reviews, they may be suitable for some people. My limited experience and the comments from many of my military friends however, suggest that they lack the comfort necessary for long-term camping.

The good news is that several suitable hammocks, designed specifically for the adventure traveler and offering a complete and safe shelter, are available for purchase. While I have used some of these hammocks, most of my reviews are based on promotional literature provided by the manufacturers and tempered by my experience. All of these hammocks should be comfortable and safe and come with bug nets and rain canopies. See the information box at the end of the chapter for specific company information.

Whether you are car camping or wilderness trekking, you should find one of these hammocks suitable for your needs.

Speer Hammock

Fully completed hammocks based on the designs in the previous chapter can be ordered from Speer Hammocks, Inc. of Marion, North Carolina. These long and wide, solid-fabric hammocks have conventional top entry and comfortably support the user's weight safely suspended below the tip-over level. A large 8X10-foot rectangular rain canopy creates a convenient stand-up shelter not found in other camping hammocks. The large canopy can be lowered for better rain and cold wind protection than other camping hammocks.

The Speer hammocks easily convert to comfortable lounge chairs and they can be deployed on the ground as conventional tarps and bivy sacks. Each hammock is customized for the user, which ensures comfort with proper length and width without excessive weight. The Speer hammocks with bug net and 8X10-foot rain canopy vary from 2 to 3 pounds. Users up to 350 pounds can be accommodated.

The removable bug net allows weight savings when it is not needed and can be left at home. Once the bug net is removed, custom-made sleeping bags conveniently slip around the hammock and provide warmth on the bottom as well as the top.

Accessories include extra wide sleep pads, radiant heat pads and sleeping bags specifically designed to go around the hammock.

Having addressed all of the issues involved in hammock camping, Speer Hammocks, Inc is the only manufacturer currently offering a complete hammock camping solution. See Appendix 1, "Advanced Features of the Speer Complete Wilderness Hammock Camping Solution" for the full details of this unique and innovative wilderness shelter.

Hennessy Hammock

The history of this hammock mirrors the rapidly expanding interest in camping hammocks. Recently introduced in the US, the Hennessy hammock now comes in different models as well as customized versions. Judging by the enthusiastic reviews of owners, this hammock is a definite winner. It is a solid-fabric hammock that safely suspends the user below the tip-over level.

Among other features, an unusual bottom entry and a removable diamond-shaped rain canopy combine to lighten the weight of this camping shelter, which varies from 1.2 to 3 pounds. A permanently attached ridgeline and bug net are included; however, these hamper the hammocks' use as a lounge chair and prevent the use of an outside sleeping bag.

The small rain canopy must be pitched close to the hammock and does not provide stand-up rain protection for someone outside the hammock.

The standard versions offer a variety of sizes and strengths to accommodate users up to 350 pounds.

Tom Hennessy of British Columbia, Canada makes this groundbreaking hammock.

The Clark Jungle Hammock

The Clark Jungle Hammock is a complete shelter and has found widespread appeal for wilderness travel. In addition to a removable rain canopy and a non-removable, zipper-attached bug net, the hammock includes bottom storage pockets and a zippered interior storm liner. It comes in three models ranging from 2.4 to 3.8 pounds and can accommodate people up to 285 pounds and 6.5 feet tall. The high-strength materials used in this hammock give the user a feeling of worry-free security.

This is a solid-fabric hammock that safely suspends the user below the tip-over level. The hammock however, is not easily used as a lounge chair or with an outside sleeping bag.

The small rain canopy must be pitched close to the hammock and does not provide stand-up rain protection for someone outside the hammock.

Gary Clark of Clark Outdoor Products, Salt Lake City, Utah makes this hammock.

Blue Ridge Camping Hammock

The Newell Hammock Company formerly sold this hammock, but in 1997 Chris Lawson and the Lawson Hammock Company of Raleigh, North Carolina acquired it. This spreader-bar hammock is one of the few that passes my comfort test. The two-section spreader bars easily support the solid-fabric hammock bottom and provide space under the permanently attached bug net and removable rain canopy. This hammock makes a roomy alternative for those who feel too confined in more traditional hammocks. It cannot however, be used as a lounge chair or with an outside sleeping bag.

The small rain canopy must be pitched close to the hammock and does not provide stand-up rain protection for someone outside the hammock.

This 4.2-pound hammock can safely hold up to 225 pounds and, when needed, easily sets up as a roomy one-man tent on the ground.

Crazy Crib

Crazy Creek Products of Red Lodge, Montana, makers of the popular camp chairs, now offer two camping hammock models, the Crazy Crib and the Crazy Crib LE. Both are complete wilderness shelters with an attached, zippered bug net and a removable rain canopy. The newest LE model features an internal sleeve that accepts a sleeping pad and keeps it in place. The one-pound basic model is 7.8 feet long by 3.7 feet wide, while the 1.94-pound LE model is 8.2 feet by 3.7 feet. The 6.4-by-8.7 foot Crazy Tarp comes with the LE model, while the basic Crazy Crib can be ordered with or without this 0.94-pound tarp. These solid fabric hammocks are constructed from sturdy materials and can be used as bivy sacks on the ground beneath the tarp.

As with many other camping hammocks, the small rain canopy must be pitched close to the hammock and does not provide stand-up rain protection for someone outside the hammock.

Dryad Hammock

The Dryad suspended sleeping shelter from Terrelogic of Toronto, Canada provides a roomy alternative to more traditional hammocks. It is essentially a tent that is suspended from its top and has a cot-type bottom supported by an aluminum-tube frame, which keeps the user level. The interior is 6.8 feet long by 2.8 feet wide and four feet high. This two-door tent/hammock has bug net sides and a removable rain fly. It weighs 6.5 pounds and can supposedly support up to 400 pounds. The Dryad cannot be used with an outside sleeping bag.

Sammock

The Sammock from Laid Back Designs, Ltd. of Ontario, Canada is a solid-fabric hammock similar to the ones above; however, it employs sectional spreader bars to provide comfort and support for its 3-by-7.5 foot size. The unique removable rain fly has built-in bug-net panels. The hammock and rain fly weigh 4.7 pounds and can support 500 pounds.

The small rain canopy is pitched close to the hammock and does not provide stand-up rain protection for someone outside the hammock.

Treeboat

Designed for tree climbers, the Treeboat is sold by New Tribe, Inc. of Grants Pass, Oregon. It is a well-made secure hammock that comes with a removable rain fly and a choice of two removable bug nets. A weather-tight tent, two types of bottom insulation, and several other items are offered as options. All four corners secure the Treeboat, which adds increased stability over most hammocks. Lightweight composite battens at each end hold the hammock open. The hammock is strong enough to hold two people, but only sleeps one comfortably. The weight of the hammock is 3.7 pounds, not counting the rain fly, bug nets, bottom insulations, and/or tent, which add considerably more weight.

Portaledge

Designed for big wall rock climbers, portaledges (suspended stretched-cot type hammocks) are manufactured by many different companies. While their sturdy construction results in weights probably too heavy for serious backpacking, they may be useful for car camping or canoe trips. Single-person portaledges generally weigh from 7 to 11 pounds, while the rain fly weighs another 3 to 4 pounds. Most do not come with bug nets. Two-person portaledges are available. For anyone interested, numerous Internet web sites providing more information about these specialized hammocks can be found by going online and searching *"portaledges"*.

Four Season Hammock

A handcrafted 100% cotton Mayan hammock is coupled with a waterproof nylon rain canopy and a mesh bug net sock for this camping system. These extremely comfortable hammocks are unique since the user sleeps sideways to the length of the hammock. It is marketed as a year-round camping system for backpacking, bicycling, paddling or snow skiing. An extreme cold-weather sleeping bag, sleep pad and waterproof-breathable bivy sack are recommended for winter use. The hammock itself weighs 1.3 pounds, however, the weights of the rain canopy, bug net and attachment ropes are not provided.

This hammock is available through Four Season Hammocks of Fort Collins, Colorado.

Siam Hammock

The Siam Hammock is made with solid nylon fabric that supports the user below the tip-over point. Plastic end rods support the zippered bug net, which is removable, allowing the hammock to be used as a lounge chair. The separate rain fly has a hood on one end and can double as a rain poncho. The hammock can be set up between supports in the traditional manner or in several tent configurations for use on the ground.

The Siam Hammock is 3.8 feet wide, 8.5 feet long, and can support up to 265 pounds. The rain fly is 5.2 feet wide and 9.8 feet long. Together they weigh 3.7 pounds.

The Siam Hammock camping system is made in Bangkok, Thailand and imported into North America by John and Lynn McConnell of J & L Merchandising in Nampa, Idaho.

Camping Hammock Manufacturers

Speer Hammocks, Inc.
34 Clear Creek Road
Marion, NC 28752-6407
828-724-4444
www.speerhammocks.com
Email: info@speerhammocks.com

Hennessy Hammock Co.
637 Southwind Road
Galiano Island, BC
Canada, V0N 1P0
888-539-2930
www.hennessyhammock.com
Email: info@hennessyhammock.com

Clark Outdoor Products
4637 South 300 West
Salt Lake City, UT 84107
800-468-4635
www.junglehammock.com
Email: info@junglehammock.com

Lawson Hammock Co.
PO Box 12602
Raleigh, NC 27605
919-829-7076
www.lawsonhammockco.com

Crazy Creek Products
PO Box 1050
1401 South Broadway
Red Lodge, MT 59068
800-331-0304
www.crazycreek.com
Email: chairs@crazycreek.com

continued

Camping Hammock Manufacturers (Cont'd.)

Terrelogic, Inc.
477 Brunswick Ave.
Toronto, Ontario
Canada, M5R 2Z6
888-693-7923
www.terrelogic.com
Email: mdj@terrelogic.com

Laid Back Designs, Ltd.
Suite 160, Unit 3
304 Stone Road
Guelph, Ontario
Canada N1G 4W4
800-465-7519
www.travelsource.com/travelstore/lbd/lbd.html
Email: sammyd@mgl.ca

New Tribe, Inc.
5517 Riverbanks Road
Grants Pass, OR 97527
866-223-3371
541-476-5804
Email: newtribe@cdsnet.net

Four Season Hammocks
1236 Oxborough Lane
Fort Collins, CO 80525
877-282-7145
Email: mrhammock@verinet.com

J & L Merchandising
52 South Grays Lane
Nampa, ID 83687
208-466-5769
www.siamhammock.com
Email: johnmac@nampa.net

Appendix 1
Advanced Features of the Speer Complete Wilderness Hammock Camping System

---

Hammock

Bug Net

Rain Canopy

Pea Pod Sleeping Bag

Sleep Pads

Hammock

1. The Speer Hammock Camping System provides unbeatable comfort and storm protection in a lightweight two- to three-pound, very convenient and highly practical wilderness shelter

2. The Hammock, Bug Net and 8X10 Rain Canopy are ready for outdoor use right from the bag; no additional items or preparation are necessary

3. The Hammock features easy and convenient top entry and exit

4. The Hammocks' great length and width provide increased comfort and security over hammocks with lesser dimensions

5. Full-length, horizontal, on-your-back sleep positions are easily possible in the Hammock

6. Curled-up, on-your-side fetal sleep positions are easily possible in the Hammock

7. The Hammock length and fabric strength can be matched to the users' physical features for greater comfort and security; two lengths accommodate users up to six feet tall and up to 6.5 feet tall, while three fabric strengths accommodate weights of less than 200 pounds, 200-250 pounds, and 250-350 pounds

8. Wide, deep sides of the occupied Hammock eliminate fears of tipping over or falling out

9. The Hammock and Bug Net easily convert to use as a bivy sack on the ground and the Rain Canopy converts to a practical tarp when necessary

10. The breathable bottom fabric helps prevent the build up of body moisture and condensation inside the Hammock

11. The bottom fabric comes with DWR treatment which helps block the entry of cold wind

12. The solid fabric bottom gives superior weight distribution that eliminates the uncomfortable pressure points that are common to ground pads, mattresses and even beds

13. The solid fabric bottom does not stretch excessively like many string net hammocks; the deep "V-shaped" sag of less-well-made hammocks is replaced by horizontal, body-contoured support which gives ergonomically-correct comfort

14. The nylon bottom fabric provides superior strength and good resistance to abrasion and rot

15. The one-piece Hammock bottom with secure end knots and strap attachments gives greater security and peace of mind versus hammocks with stitched seams

16. Spray-on vapor-proof treatments can be conveniently added to, and later removed from the bottom fabric as needed to adjust to seasonal temperatures

17. The dependable, full-length Velcro hook and loop attachments for the Bug Net allow quick hassle-free entry and/or exit on either side of the Hammock

18. The extra-long (12') hanging straps allow setup between wide supports, thus providing increased comfort over hammocks with short hanging straps

19. The polypropylene hanging straps are strong and have low-memory stretch; they can easily be adjusted for the proper tension

20. The wide hanging straps protect the bark of young trees

21. The four-wrap "non-knot" recommended for attaching the hanging straps to the trees offers great ease of use and avoids damage to the trees

22. If necessary, bandanas or extra socks can be tied to the Hammock hanging straps to stop rain water from seeping along the straps and into the Hammock

23. Velcro loop attachment strips are used on the Hammock edges to reduce entanglements with clothes or fleece fabrics

24. Wet or sweaty clothes can be hung to dry from the Hammock hanging straps

25. Large personal items, such as water bottles, boots, journal, books, sweater, etc., can be placed on the ground beneath the Hammock for easy access

Bug Net

26. The Bug Net can be opened on either side of the Hammock for easy entry and exit

27. The large, full-length Bug Net with No-See-Um netting provides ample protection from mosquitoes, black flies and even smaller biting gnats

28. The Bug Net is removable and can be left at home when not needed for a weight savings of six ounces

29. The removable Bug Net allows the innovative use of a Sleeping Bag completely around the Hammock for greater warmth than inside use

30. The removable Bug Net allows the Hammock to be used as a convenient and comfortable lounge chair

31. The long-life 100% polyester Bug Net fabric provides superior outdoor use

32. The black Bug Net fabric provides improved visibility for the Hammock user (who is close to the netting) while providing greater privacy (reduced visibility by distant observers)

33. The Bug Net support line is extra long to accommodate varying Hammock setups

34. The Bug Net support line is a stiff cord (solid core with nylon sheath, like climbing rope); it is strong (275 lb), lightweight, and tangle-free

35. The Bug Net support line is bright pink for increased visibility in low light conditions

36. The Bug Net support line is adjustable by the Hammock occupant for optimum interior space with each setup

37. Small personal items, such as eyeglasses, flashlight, pen, bandana, etc., can be hung from the Bug Net support line for easy use inside the Hammock

38. The Bug Net support line can be loosened and moved aside to allow the Hammock to be used as a lounge chair

39. The Bug Net support line can be loosened and hung beneath the Hammock to accommodate the use of the Pea Pod Sleeping Bag

40. The Bug Net support line can be completely removed when it is not needed and can be left at home for weight savings

41. Full-length "finger-tabs" on the inner Hammock edges allow quick and easy separation of the Bug Net by the occupant, even in complete darkness

42. Velcro hook attachment strips are used on the Bug Net edges where they are less likely to entangle clothes or fleece fabrics

Rain Canopy

43. The extra large 8X10 Rain Canopy is separate from the Hammock and extends well beyond the Hammock itself

44. The Rain Canopy can be set up high enough to provide a convenient stand-up shelter that is not available with other camp shelters

45. The Rain Canopy is large enough to allow the user to enter/exit the Hammock, or even cook a meal on the ground during a rain storm without getting wet

46. The Rain Canopy is made from lightweight, yet strong, 1.1 oz/yd^2 silicone-coated ripstop nylon

47. The Rain Canopy is made from mood-enhancing natural colors for greater comfort in prolonged fowl-weather conditions

48. The Rain Canopy is made with reinforced seams and pull tabs for added strength and security

49. The central seam on the Rain Canopy is factory sealed for waterproof-ness

50. Six ten-foot guidelines are included with the Rain Canopy and provide adequate tie outs for most outdoor situations

51. The Rain Canopy can easily be lowered closer to the Hammock for greater rain and/or wind protection when necessary

52. Four extra pull tabs on the Rain Canopy allow attachment of additional tie outs when needed in high-wind conditions

53. The Rain Canopy guidelines are strong (275 lb), yet lightweight stiff cord (solid core with nylon sheath, like climbing ropes)

54. The Rain Canopy guidelines are no-tangle for ease of use in actual outdoor situations

55. The extra-long guidelines allow easy set up of the Rain Canopy when used over the Hammock between trees or when used on the ground as a conventional tarp

56. Grommets on the two ridge pull tabs of the Rain Canopy facilitate set up on the ground by readily accepting the tips of most hiking poles when they are used upside down as tarp poles

57. Wet or sweaty clothes can be hung to dry from the Rain Canopy guidelines

Pea Pod Sleeping Bag

58. The Pea Pod Sleeping Bag is designed to encircle the Hammock for complete warmth without compressing the insulation on the bottom

59. The Pea Pod Sleeping Bag is made from strong lightweight (1.1 oz/yd^2) ripstop nylon with durable-water-resistant (DWR) finish

60. The DWR coating on the Pea Pod Sleeping Bag effectively blocks cold wind without trapping excess body moisture in the insulation

61. The Pea Pod Sleeping Bag comes with synthetic insulation for superior light weight and warmth

62. The Pea Pod Sleeping Bag is made extra long and with greater girth to eliminate the loss of insulating loft common to sleeping bags not designed to go around the Hammock

63. The Pea Pod Sleeping Bag has draw-cord closures at each end and hook and loop fasteners on the long edges which allow it to easily fit around the Hammock

64. The Pea Pod Sleeping Bag can be used as a regular enclosed sleeping bag or it can be unfolded completely flat for use as a blanket

65. Full-length "finger-tabs" on the long edges of the Pea Pod Sleeping Bag allow quick and easy entry and exit, even in complete darkness

66. The Pea Pod Sleeping Bag is made with light-colored inside fabric for improved radiant heat performance

67. The Pea Pod Sleeping Bag is made with dark-colored outside fabric for improved heat absorption (and evaporation of inside moisture) when drying in the sun

68. The Pea Pod Sleeping Bag can be used alone around the Hammock or in combination with extra clothes, sleep pad/s, fleece blankets, or traditional sleeping bags inside the Hammock as dictated by the outside temperature

69. The Pea Pod Sleeping Bag can easily be worn as a robe with one's head and feet projecting through the end openings. This saves weight and bulk by eliminating the need for warm camp clothes

Sleep Pads

70. Extra wide (24-40 in) Sleep Pads serve as liners inside the Hammock and provide superior comfort and warmth versus the narrower pads generally used for ground sleeping

71. The Speer Sleep Pad is thin (1/4" or 5/16") to avoid the uncomfortable folds and bulges common to thick pads when used in the curved world of the Hammock

72. The Speer Sleep Pads can be used alone or in combination with other narrower or thicker pads for added warmth

73. The Speer radiant-heat Sleep Pads block the escape of much of the body's radiant heat

Make your own camp heaven

Appendix 2
Tips for Hammock Camping

Advantages Of Hammock Camping

Selecting A Hammock Campsite

Setting Up A Speer Hammock

Staying Warm In A Speer Hammock

Making A Speer Hammock

Buying A Hammock

Some Safety Do's and Don'ts

Advantages Of Hammock Camping

- When properly fit, they are far more comfortable than ground beds
- Complete shelter with bug net and rain canopy
- Large 8X10-foot rain canopy makes a stand up shelter with a bed fit for a king
- Reduced tossing and turning
- Horizontal back- and fetal-sleep positions are possible
- Reduced back discomfort
- No more crawling around on the ground to make camp
- Ultra lightweight
- Adequate rain and storm protection
- Make/break camp in rain w\o pack items getting wet
- Adjust canopy for fair or foul weather
- Unlimited campsites in forested terrain
- Greater freedom than using tents or tarps
- Generally takes only minutes to find a campsite
- Sleep above rocks or roots
- Sleep above briers, cactus, poison oak, etc.
- Quick set up and take down
- Use as lounge chair
- Avoid snakes
- Avoid slugs and spiders
- Avoid sleeping on the hard ground, rocks or roots typical of many tent or tarp sites
- Avoid sleeping on wet or uneven ground
- Avoid crowded or abused campsites
- Hide from cold wind behind mountain ridges
- Avoid storm-exposed campsites
- Camp at bug-free sites
- Camp at scenic sites
- Camp at sites with sunset or sunrise views
- Camp out of sight
- Avoid the food-robbing critters that are common at the usual ground campsites
- Avoid high-risk bear territory by camping in low-risk habitats unsuitable for tents or tarps

- Avoid ground mice and rats
- Camp in greater peace and harmony with nature
- Use as tarp and bivy sack on the ground when no trees are available or temperatures drop
- Convenient way to follow Leave No Trace camping ethics
- Can be custom made for any camper's height or weight

Selecting A Hammock Campsite

- Avoid cold wind by camping on the lee side of hills, ridges or cliffs
- Camp on steep rugged mountainsides
- Camp on mountaintops with no suitable tent or tarp sites
- Camp on cliff tops
- Camp at base of cliffs, even in the midst of large breakdown boulders
- Camp deep in the forest
- Camp on rocky, brushy, wet or uneven ground
- Avoid camping near springs, streams or lakes
- Camp far from water sources by making dinner before stopping and making a dry camp
- Camp in windy spots to keep bugs away
- Avoid wet buggy tent or tarp sites by finding dry bug-free sites
- Camp off the beaten track and out of sight
- Camp close to towns without being seen or disturbed
- Camp miles from the nearest tent campsite
- Continue traveling until dark or later, knowing you can easily make camp anywhere only moments after deciding to do so
- Avoid worry of finding campsites already occupied
- Set up camp easily and quickly when bad weather strikes
- Avoid setting up in areas prone to heavy dew, such as open grassy meadows on cold windless nights

where all objects above the ground, including the hammock, will collect excessive condensation

Setting Up A Speer Hammock

- Select sturdy supports, such as trees, rocks, etc
- Trees should be at least 4" in diameter
- Select support spacing of 12-16'; generally 4-6 paces between trees
- Avoid tree damage by using flat webbing instead of round ropes
- Avoid tree damage by using overlapping 4-wrap knots
- If forced to tie a knot in a hanging strap, insert a stick or a large loop of the free end of the strap into the knot to facilitate untying it later
- Loosen the bug net support line before pitching the hammock
- Position 2-4' of hanging strap on each end of hammock
- Attach hanging straps at same height above ground for level hammock
- Set up on sloping ground often requires tree knots at different heights above the ground in order for hammock to be level
- Before occupying hammock, step back and visibly judge if it is level; readjust setup if necessary
- Shorten one hanging strap or raise/lower one hanging strap tree knot to adjust pitch of hammock
- Leave some sag in unoccupied hammock; do not stretch tight
- Adjust comfort by readjusting setup if necessary
- Adjust interior space below bug net by readjusting the support line after the hammock is occupied
- To make camp in rain, set up canopy first
- To break camp in rain, take down canopy last
- Use socks or bandanas to stop rain from seeping along hanging straps and reaching hammock

- For lounge chair, hang bug net and bug net support line out of the way over the back side of the hammock
- Remove bug net and bug net support line to save weight in winter
- When bugs are not a problem, remove bug net for enhanced harmony with nature and better star views
- Stow personal items like eyeglasses, wrist watches, flashlights, bandanas, etc. by hanging them from the bug net support line inside the hammock
- Stow larger items like water bottle, shoes/boots, book/map, jacket, etc. within reach on ground beneath hammock
- Hang backpack from hammock strap so it is beneath the rain canopy and does not touch the ground
- When in porcupine country, hang shoes or boots from hammock straps; leave nothing on the ground
- Hang wet or soiled clothing from hammock straps or rain canopy guidelines
- Use 4-wrap knots for hammock and rain canopy as described in Chapter 1 to ensure canopy is centered over hammock
- In high wind or stormy conditions, make sure all lines are tied tight; use extra pull tabs on rain canopy

Staying Warm In A Speer Hammock

- Use the Pea Pod Sleeping Bag completely around the hammock to avoid crushing insulation on bottom!
- Hide from cold wind behind ridges, hills, cliffs, etc.
- Use layering system (sleeping bag, sleep pad, clothes, blanket, jacket, vapor barrier bag, etc.)
- Use sleeping bags and sleep pads as needed
- Wear sleeping bag over you as a blanket
- Use pile and/or fleece clothing, liner, or blanket
- Use light colored fabrics for reflection of radiant heat

- Wind/water proof hammock bottom for cold wind, then remove when warm temperatures return
- Use aluminized fabrics to block 97% of radiant heat loss, but watch for excessive condensation
- Choose sleep pads greater than 22" wide
- Avoid extremely wide and thick sleep pads since they tend to buckle and create uncomfortable bulges
- Use closed-cell foam pads (generally 1/4 to 5/8" thick)
- Use foam-or down-filled inflatable sleep pads (generally 1 to 3" thick)
- Use aluminum-covered bubble wrap sleep pads (windshield sunscreens or Reflectix sheets cut to size)
- Watch for excessive condensation of body moisture with all sleep pads
- Switch to 1" thick sleep pad when temperatures drop below about 40°F
- Avoid slippery sleep pads that shift underneath you; inexpensive non-slippery foam pads are available
- Wear all available clothing in sleeping bag; be careful with non-breathable fabrics
- Use vapor barrier bag or liner **inside** sleeping bag
- Use Aluminized Mylar sheet (emergency or survival blankets) between hammock and Pea Pod Sleeping Bag (beware possible excessive condensation)
- To avoid suffocation, never use vapor barrier over your face
- Wear rain/wind suit over underwear inside sleeping bag for make-shift vapor barrier bag
- Avoid all vapor barriers (including all waterproof/breathable fabrics) on the **outside** of sleeping bag since they will trap excessive body condensation
- Most good quality sleeping bags already have DWR treatments on outer fabric for effective wind blocking

- Do not wear all available clothing inside vapor barrier bag or everything will be soaked the next morning
- If using a vapor barrier bag, have some dry clothing to put on in the morning
- Vent your breath outside, not inside the sleeping bag
- Air dry your sleeping bag as much as possible every day since body moisture accumulates in it every night
- Eat nutritious, easily-digested food for calories to burn for warmth
- Eat just before going to bed; use sleep-robbing sugar or caffeine sparingly
- Snack during the night for calories to burn for warmth
- Avoid dehydration by drinking **lots** of water day and night
- When the gear you have is not enough to keep you warm--try sleeping on the ground, returning to the comfort of the hammock as soon as warmer temperatures return

Making A Speer Hammock

- Making your own hammock is simple and fun
- Costs about $100 and, with materials in hand, takes 1-2 days
- All fabrics and materials can be mail ordered
- You will need a regular sewing machine and only minimal sewing skills
- Use regular needles and 100% polyester thread
- Avoid cotton or cotton-covered polyester thread since it absorbs water and quickly rots in outdoor environments
- Use breathable hammock bottoms to reduce buildup of body moisture in sleeping bag
- Choose strong, low-stretch, sun- and rot-resistant nylon fabrics for hammock bottom

174 - Hammock Camping

- If you are less than 200 pounds: use 1.9 oz/yd² ripstop or 70 denier 2.2 oz/yd² taffeta and 1"-wide polypropylene webbing straps
- If you are between 200 and 250 pounds: use Supplex in 2.5 to 3.5 oz/yd² weights and 1"-wide polypropylene webbing straps
- If you are between 250 and 350 pounds: use Cordura in 3.5 to 4.5 oz/yd² weights and 1.5"-wide polypropylene webbing straps
- Choose light natural colors for better radiant heat retention than dark colors
- Inexpensive discount fabrics may be locally available
- Interior hammock length should be your height plus 2'
- Hammock width should be 5'
- Except for hems, do not sew hammock fabric; use single piece to avoid catastrophic failure due to needle-hole weakened fabric along seams
- Tie overhand end knots on each end of hammock fabric
- Allow extra fabric for hammock end knots (24-30")
- Use 1.1 oz/yd² silicone-coated ripstop nylon for the rain canopy
- Large 8' X 10' rain canopy provides convenient stand-up shelter
- Rain canopy is made from two 5' X 8' fabric pieces, joined by a central seam to get finished 8' X 10' size
- Use reinforced "flat felled" seam to join the two rain canopy panels
- Rain canopy central seam must be waterproofed
- Inexpensive silicone seam sealant can be made from solvent and household silicone caulking
- Make sure guidelines on rain canopy are 10' long for set up over the hanging hammock or as a tarp on the ground
- Avoid limp guidelines on rain canopy since they tangle badly
- Use 1/16" Pulse Line for guidelines since they are low-tangle, lightweight, strong and highly visible
- Install at least ten pull tabs on the rain canopy to allow for secure set up, even in strong wind

- Install grommets on the rain canopy's ridgeline pull tabs to allow convenient use of most hiking poles as tarp supports when set up on the ground (use hiking poles upside down)
- Use no-see-um bug netting for complete bug protection
- Bug net is held by an adjustable bug net support line; readjust it for each setup
- Use 1.0 oz/yd^2 100% polyester no-see-um bug netting
- Use black bug netting for best see-through feature from inside hammock
- Avoid mosquito netting which will allow small biting gnats to pass through
- Attach bug net to hammock with hook and loop fasteners for hassle-free, dependable entry and exit
- Bug net should be completely removable
- Use low-memory stretch, strong, non-water absorbent and rot-resistant polypropylene webbing for hammock straps
- Be sure to choose good quality polypropylene webbing with tensile strength of at least 600 lbs/in.
- Some 1" wide polypropylene webbing is not strong enough, ask before buying
- Avoid nylon webbing for hammock straps due to its' excessive high-memory stretch
- Attach hanging straps to hammock by sewing a loop in each strap at each hammock end knot
- Avoid tying tight knots in hammock straps since they weaken the strap at the knots themselves
- Properly reinforced stitching is stronger than knots in the straps

Buying A Hammock

- Choose a solid fabric hammock for proper suspension, weight distribution, comfort and safety
- Choose a hammock with bug net and rain canopy

- Choose a hammock with an extra large rain canopy for dependable, convenient and secure wilderness use
- Consider a hammock with a rain canopy large enough to offer storm protection when pitched as stand-up shelter
- Military-type jungle hammocks may lack the comfort necessary for long-term use
- String net hammocks may lack long-term comfort
- Avoid hammocks with spreader bars if they raise the user too close to the tip-over point
- Avoid or return any hammock that tips over or feels like it will
- Consider the weight of hammock, rain canopy and bug net; heavy units may be inappropriate for uses like long-distance hiking
- Study the reviews in Chapter 7, "How To Buy a Hammock"
- Review manufactures literature including the Internet sites given in Chapter 7 and Appendix 3
- Some hammocks may come with rain canopies that lack guidelines or require additional waterproofing
- Remember, hammock comfort in general is dependent on length. Longer is more comfortable, so avoid short hammocks
- Choose a hammock with interior length at least 2 feet longer than your height for best comfort (stretched-cot type hammocks may not need this extra length)
- For safety, choose a hammock suitable for your weight
- For serious wilderness use, consider a hammock that also conveniently sets up on the ground as a tarp and bivy sack
- Consider a hammock with removable bug net for the increased-warmth use of a sleeping bag around the hammock
- Consider a removable bug net for using the hammock as a lounge chair
- Consider a removable bug net for weight savings during bug-free season

- Consider a removable rain canopy for improved views when not needed
- Consider the actual usefulness of extra items like interior pockets, bottom pockets, interior pad retainers, wind shells, bottom entry, zippers, etc.
- Some extra features may be desirable for some uses, for instance car camping, cabin or backyard users may not be as concerned about weight and storm protection as long-term wilderness trekkers
- Hammocks for children may need extra material strength for safety

Some Safety Do's and Don'ts

- Avoid falling out by staying low in the hammock
- Beware of spreader bars that raise the body to the tip-over point
- Avoid catastrophic failure of the hammock materials
- Inspect each hammock setup for incipient failure
- Avoid or repair any damaged hammock
- Repeatedly inspect hanging knots to avoid surprises
- Avoid tying to dead trees or other supports that could fail
- Avoid overhead dead branches or tree tops that could fall
- Avoid overhead snow-covered branches
- Set up the hammock at waist height or lower to facilitate safe entry and exit
- Exercise caution getting in or out of hammock to avoid loss of balance
- For better control when entering or exiting, hold the hammock with both hands, one on each side of the hammock
- Avoid sunlight as much as possible to prevent deterioration of nylon and polypropylene materials
- Avoid tripping over the canopy guidelines
- Avoid walking into the hammock tie-outs

- Avoid entanglements in the hammock materials
- Wash the hammock and bug net as needed
- Limit hammock use to one person at a time
- Do not exceed the design weight limit
- Do not swing in the hammock
- Avoid sudden heavy movements in the hammock
- Avoid punctures, tears or rips to the hammock fabric
- Possible puncture problems exist inside the hammock from wristwatches, belt buckles, boots, shoes, eyeglasses, ear phones, portable radios, zippers on sleeping bag or clothes, writing pens, flashlights, etc.
- Avoid snagging the hammock fabric on brush, limbs, briers, rocks, etc. while making or breaking camp
- Avoid open flames; the hammock materials are flammable
- Do not smoke in the hammock
- Restrict and supervise children's use of the hammock
- Do not leave infants unattended in the hammock
- The physically handicapped may have difficulties in the hammock
- Use a whistle if you set up far from the traveled path but need to attract the attention of others for help
- Avoid contact with poisonous plants, including vines on trees; even dead plants/vines can cause problems
- Do not completely enclose the Pea Pod Sleeping Bag; instead avoid suffocation and the buildup of excessive moisture in the insulation by leaving a large space for fresh air and the escape of your exhaled breath
- Avoid high-risk situations susceptible to storm dangers such as lighting, excessive winds or flooding

Appendix 3
Online Hammock Resources

---

www.HammockCamping.com

Camping Hammock Manufacturers

General Use Hammock Manufacturers and Merchants

History of Hammocks

Camping Hammock Use

How to Make Your Own Hammock

Suppliers of Fabrics and Materials for Making Hammocks

www.HammockCamping.com

This is a full feature web site devoted to hammock camping. Excerpts from the book *Hammock Camping, The Complete Guide to Greater Comfort, Convenience and Freedom* are included.

Camping Hammock Manufacturers

The following is a list of manufacturers that make and sell camping hammocks (only secure, comfortable and complete hammocks with bug net and rain canopy are included).

Speer Hammocks, Inc.
34 Clear Creek Road
Marion, NC 28752-6407
828-724-4444
www.speerhammocks.com
Email: info@speerhammocks.com

Hennessy Hammock Co.
637 Southwind Road
Galiano Island, BC
Canada, V0N 1P0
888-539-2930
www.hennessyhammock.com
Email: info@hennessyhammock.com

Clark Outdoor Products
4637 South 300 West
Salt Lake City, UT 84107
800-468-4635
www.junglehammock.com
Email: info@junglehammock.com

Lawson Hammock Co.
PO Box 12602
Raleigh, NC 27605
919-829-7076
www.lawsonhammockco.com
www.tbcinc.com/hammocks/hamindex.html

Crazy Creek Products

PO Box 1050
1401 South Broadway
Red Lodge, MT 59068
800-331-0304
www.crazycreek.com
Email: chairs@crazycreek.com

Terrelogic, Inc.

477 Brunswick Ave.
Toronto, Ontario
Canada, M5R 2Z6
888-693-7923
www.terrelogic.com
Email: mdj@terrelogic.com

Laid Back Designs, Ltd.

Suite 160, Unit 3
304 Stone Road
Guelph, Ontario
Canada N1G 4W4
800-465-7519
travelsource.com/travelstore/lbd/lbd.html
Email: sammyd@mgl.ca

New Tribe, Inc.

5517 Riverbanks Road
Grants Pass, OR 97527
866-223-3371
541-476-5804
Email: newtribe@cdsnet.net

Four Season Hammocks

1236 Oxborough Lane
Fort Collins, CO 80525
877-282-7145
Email: mrhammock@verinet.com

Siam Hammock

Tawatchai Jaranai (Eff)
80/2 Prachachuen Road 33
Ladyao Jatujak Bangkok 10900 Thailand
+66-1869-8988
www.siamhammock.com
Email: f_goodfeeling@yahoo.com

General Use Hammock Manufactures and Merchants

This list contains some Internet merchants and sources of general use hammocks. Some sites must be searched in order to find the hammock information.

International Hammocks

www.hameck.com
www.exotichammocks.com
www.hangouts.com
www.bstreethomeandgarden.com
www.hammocks.org
www.swingsnthings.com
www.houseofhammocks.com
www.backyardamerica.com
www.outdoorfurnitureonline.com
www.shopoutdoordecor.com
laatc.hypermart.net/hammocks.html
www.milemarker0.com/hammocks.htm
www.campmor.com
www.hammocks.com
www.ticketothemoon.com

North American Hammocks

www.onlinesports.com
www.backcountrygear.com
www.indoorsandoutdoors.com
www.bayhammocks.com
www.hammockking.com
www.algonquinhammocks.com
www.comfortchannel.com/orhatham.htm
www.keywesthammocks.com
www.nagshead.com
www.HatHam.com
www.carolinaswingcompany.com
www.webhammock.com
www.twinoakstore.com
www.nchammock.com
www.unclejoes.com
www.jpaul.com
www.outerbankshammocks.com
www.way2coolgifts.com
www.theoutdoorworld.com

South American Hammocks
    www.aztecart.co.uk
    www.hammocks.net
    www.hamaca.com
    www.hammockdream.com
    www.nicamaka.com
    www.vorcom.com

Military Hammocks
    www.armynavymilitarysurplus.com
    www.tedsmilitarysurplus.com
    www.mitchells.net.au

History of Hammocks

These sites offer some interesting information on the history and development of hammock use in the world.

    www.ecomall.com/greenshopping/hammock.htm
    www.hammocks.net/hammock-history.html

Camping Hammock Use

Helpful information and tips on backcountry camping in hammocks can be found at these sites.

    www.hammockcamping.com
    www.treehanger.com
    www.shire.net/mormon/hammock.html

How to Make Your Own Hammock

Helpful information on making your own camping hammock can be found at these sites.

> **www.speerhammocks.com**
> **www.hammockcamping.com**
> **www.shelter-systems.com/gripclips/**
> **hammock.html**

Suppliers of Fabrics and Materials for Making Hammocks

The following list contains mail-order suppliers of camping hammock fabrics and materials useful in making your own hammock.

American Home & Habitat
10400 Courthouse Rd. PMB 274
Spotsylvania, VA 22553
540-710-9249
www.americanhomeandhabitat.com
Email: info@americanhomeandhabitat.com

Emerald Citi Textile, Inc.
3322 16th St.
Everett, WA 98201
888-343-1220
www.ectextile.com
Email: info@ectextile.com

Outdoor Threads
1808 Belmont Ave.
Hood River, OR 97031
541-386-5445
www.outdoorthreads.com
Email: slaes@outdoorthreads.com

Outdoor Wilderness Fabrics, Inc.
16415 Midland Blvd.
Nampa, ID 83687
800-693-7467
www.owfinc.com
Email: owfinc@owfinc.com

Quest Outfitters
4919 Hubner
Sarasota, FL 34241
800-359-6931
www.questoutfitters.com
Email: questoutfitters@home.com

Seattle Fabrics, Inc.
8702 Aurora Ave. N
Seattle, WA 98103
206-525-0670
www.seattlefabrics.com

Textile Outfitters
735 10th Ave. SW
Calgary, AB
Canada T2R 0B3
403-543-7677
www.justmakeit.com
Email: moreinfo@justmakeit.com

The Rain Shed, Inc.
707 NW 11th
Corvallis, OR 97330
541-753-8900

186 - Hammock Camping

Using a hammock can change your view of the world

Appendix 4
Leave No Trace
Camping

 The Leave No Trace Principles of Outdoor
Ethics:

1. **Plan Ahead and Prepare**
2. **Travel and Camp on Durable Surfaces**
3. **Dispose of Waste Properly**
4. **Leave What You Find**
5. **Minimize Campfire Impacts**
6. **Respect Wildlife**
7. **Be Considerate of Other Visitors**

Leave No Trace, Inc. is a national non-profit
organization dedicated to promoting and inspiring
outdoor recreation through education, research and
partnerships. Leave No Trace builds awareness,
appreciation and respect for our wild lands.

The Leave No Trace program is designed to assist
visitors with their decisions when they travel and camp
on America's public lands. The program strives to
educate visitors about the nature of their recreational

impacts as well as techniques to prevent and minimize such impacts. Leave No Trace is best understood as an educational and ethical program, not as a set of rules and regulations.

The non-political mission of Leave No Trace is to promote and inspire responsible outdoor recreation through education, research and partnerships. The program is focused specifically on human-powered (non-motorized) recreation.

Imagine what it would be like if every outdoor user followed the Leave No Trace Principles of Outdoor Ethics:

Plan Ahead and Prepare
- Know the regulations and special concerns for the area you'll visit.
- Prepare for extreme weather, hazards, and emergencies.
- Schedule your trip to avoid times of high use.
- Visit in small groups. Split larger parties into groups of 4 to 6.
- Repackage food to minimize waste.
- Use a map and compass to eliminate the use of marking paint, rock cairns or flagging.

Travel and Camp on Durable Surfaces
- Durable surfaces include established trails and campsites, rock, gravel, dry grasses or snow.
- Protect riparian areas by camping at least 200 feet from lakes and streams.
- Good campsites are found, not made. Altering a site is not necessary.
- In popular areas:
  - Concentrate use on existing trails and campsites.
  - Walk single file in the middle of the trail, even when wet or muddy.

- Keep campsites small. Focus activity in areas where vegetation is absent.
- In pristine areas:
  - Disperse use to prevent the creation of campsites and trails.
  - Avoid places where impacts are just beginning.

Dispose of Waste Properly
- Pack it in, pack it out. Inspect your campsite and rest areas for trash or spilled foods. Pack out all trash, leftover food, and litter.
- Deposit solid human waste in cat holes dug 6 to 8 inches deep at least 200 feet from water, camp, and trails. Cover and disguise the cat hole when finished.
- Pack out toilet paper and hygiene products.
- To wash yourself or your dishes, carry water 200 feet away from streams or lakes and use small amounts of biodegradable soap. Scatter strained dishwater.

Leave What You Find
- Preserve the past: examine, but do not touch, cultural or historic structures and artifacts.
- Leave rocks, plants and other natural objects as you find them.
- Avoid introducing or transporting non-native species.
- Do not build structures, furniture, or dig trenches.

Minimize Campfire Impacts
- Campfires can cause lasting impacts to the backcountry. Use a lightweight stove for cooking and enjoy a candle lantern for light.
- Where fires are permitted, use established fire rings, fire pans, or mound fires.

- Keep fires small, Only use sticks from the ground that can be broken by hand.
- Burn all wood and coals to ash, put out campfires completely, then scatter cool ashes.

Respect Wildlife

- Observe wildlife from a distance. Do not follow or approach them.
- Never feed animals. Feeding wildlife damages their health, alters natural behaviors, and exposes them to predators and other dangers.
- Protect wildlife and your food by storing rations and trash securely.
- Control pets at all times, or leave them at home.
- Avoid wildlife during sensitive times: mating, nesting, raising young, or winter.

Be Considerate of Other Visitors

- Respect other visitors and protect the quality of their experience.
- Be courteous. Yield to other users on the trail.
- Step to the downhill side of the trail when encountering pack stock.
- Take breaks and camp away from trails and other visitors.
- Let nature's sounds prevail. Avoid loud voices and noises.

Contact Leave No Trace at the following address or visit them online at **www.LNT.org** to learn even more ways of reducing your impact on the outdoors. Join and support this worthy organization. Best of all, make sure you set a good example by your own outdoor ethics.

LEAVE NO TRACE
PO Box 997
Boulder, CO 80306
fax: 303-442-8217
phone: 303-442-8222

Take a hammock instead of a tent
The earth and your bones will thank you

192 - Hammock Camping

I've seen the seasons stand their ground,
  The flooding rivers stage.
I've seen the mountains blush with fear,
  Afore the thunderous rage.
I've seen the shadows run their course,
  Across the meadows green.
I've seen the warm sun cast its spell,
  With all its magic sheen.
I've seen the morning dew encase,
  The primal cove and glen.
I've heard the glad voice of the lark,
  The warble of the wren.
I've watched the breeze stir up the trees,
  To gay melodic song.
And on that wind, God's gentle hand,
  To carry me along.
In sun, in rain, storm-laden days,
  They're all the same to me.
No doubt, you'll make no sense of it,
  A baffling mystery.
But where the mountains part the sky,
  Here joy and peace prevail.
The face of God I see...as He
  All earthly cares assail.
And by these temples where I rest,
  The Lord takes care of me.
There is not one thing that I lack,
  I've true serenity.
And so, you think I am poor,
  And want for sheltered home.
But here in God I trust my fate,
  ...For I am not alone.

Nimblewill Nomad "GOING HOME"

Index

Quick Order Form

Hammock Camping

No Risk Money Back Guarantee

Fax orders: 828-724-4444, call first. Send this form

Telephone orders: Call 828-724-4444 Have your credit card ready

Email orders: info@SpeerHammocks.com

Postal orders: Speer Hammocks, PO Box 34-D Clear Creek Road, Marion, NC 28752-6407, USA. Telephone: 828-724-4444

Name: _____

Address: _____

City: _____State: _____Zip: _____

Telephone: _____

Email address: _____

$19.95 US each book   # of books ordered _____ $ _____
Plus shipping via Priority Mail
    US: $5.00 for first book; $3.00 each additional book.............$ _____
    International: $9.00 for first book; $5.00 each
        additional book (estimate).......................................$ _____
NC residents add $1.30 sales tax...................................$ _____
Total amount of order ....$ _____

Payment: Check/Money Order_____ payable to Speer Hammocks, Inc.

      Credit Card: Visa_____   MasterCard_____

Card number: _____

Expiration Date (MM/YY): _____

Name on card: _____